I0890121

The Ancient History of U Thong

city of gold

ANNA BENNETT

A SCIENTIFIC STUDY OF THE GOLD FROM U THONG

Published by DASTA and BIA
Distributed by River Books
396 Maharaj Road, Tatien, Bangkok
T: (66 2) 622-1900, 224-6686
F: (66 2) 225-3861
E: order@riverbooksbk.com
www.riverbooksbk.com

ISBN 978 616 7339 81 8

Edited by Ian Glover and Peter Skilling
Proof readers Ian Glover, Peter Skilling and David Weldon
Layout by Anna Bennett, Pairot Singbun Manager of SuthiRatana Foundation and Marine Penhouet
Satellite Maps by Geo-Informatics and Space Technology Development Agency (Public Organization) Gistda

Printed and bound in Thailand by Sirivatana Interprint Public Company Limited.

BIA DASTA

CONTENTS

I would like to dedicate this publication to Phuthorn Bhumadhon

DASTA FOREWORD

Designated Area of U Thong Ancient City is one in six areas under the Designated Areas for Sustainable Tourism Administration (Public Organization) or DASTA with distinctive characteristics. It is a designated area continuously visited and surveyed by scholars and those interested in history and archaeology, at national and international levels, since U Thong Ancient City is the site with numerous important archaeological evidence accepted in history and archaeology academic circles around the world. Several archaeological evidence are important indicators of traces of Buddhism and ancient human civilizations, including ancient golden utensils and ornaments discovered in Designated Area of U Thong Ancient City, from archaeological excavations carried out by the Department of Fine Arts, presently kept at U Thong National Museum.

DASTA realizes the importance of ancient gold in U Thong Ancient City with important archaeological evidence that has not been studied and researched in detail by specialized experts. DASTA has therefore joined Buddhadasa Indapanno Archives Foundation in consultation and coordination to invite Dr. Anna T. Bennett, a world expert on ancient gold to join the study and research of U Thong ancient gold with modern scientific method, under the international research study and workshop project on Golden Objects of U Thong by the World Expert on Ancient Gold from London.

It is DASTA's fervent hope that the research project on ancient gold in Thailand's golden land: U Thong, Suphanburi, will be a research work that yields valuable data, benefitting history and archaeology academic circles at national, regional and international levels, including those involved with participatory process in developing Designated Area of U Thong Ancient City and interested public members. Moreover, this research work will be further propagated at the world arena, and can be referred to in extended history and archaeology studies as well as development for Thailand's sustainable tourism in the future.

BIA FOREWORD

What is Suvarnabhumi? Where was it located? Did it really exist? Although the answers to these questions have, until now, not yet been concluded. Suvarnabhumi is highly important in the history and legend of Buddhism in all sects and schools whether in India-Sri Lanka, Southeast Asia, East Asian countries - China, Japan, and Korea, including the Middle East and areas around the Mediterranean Sea. Suvarnabhumi was mentioned in jataka tales, mantras, antecedents, legends, and various records as a rich and fertile land, the land in Southeast Asia where Buddhism was first and firmly established. There have been numbers of research work conducted in various countries in order to precisely locate Suvarnabhumi, especially In Thailand where some cities and the kingdom bear names that are similar to Suvarnabhumi such as Suphanabhumi, Suphanburi, Kanchanaburi, and U Thong.

The BIA was approached by the Designated Areas for Sustainable Tourism Administration (Public Organization) or DASTA to conduct a study titled "U Thong awaits its revival...through the trace of beads and early Buddhism in the basin of the rivers: Mae Klong and Ta Chine." It was the area where evidence of 'gold' was found but no scientific analysis has yet been conducted. Due to the disscussion with the Deputy Director of DASTA at that time, Mrs. Sirikul Kasivivat and Mr. Phnombootra Chandrajoti, the Director of U Thong National Museum, it was agreed that a study which would involve scientific analysis may be a key to the unanswered questions. Dr. Anna Bennett, an archaeologist and metallurgist who is internationally known as an expert analyst in these fields graciously agreed to conduct this study unconditionally. When she was a student at the University of London 32 years ago, Dr. Bennett visited Thailand to join the archaeological excavation at Ban Don Ta Phet and conducted the exhibition in U Thong National Museum. Since then she has formed a bond with Thailand and friendship with many Thai people. While conducting this most recent study, she received kind support from the staff members of U Thong National Museum and the National Museum in Bangkok. The administrators and officers of DASTA both in the central office and U Thong and SuthiRatana Foundation were also extremely helpful. In addition, Khun Lek Suriya at U Thong were especially generous for bringing their private collections for the analysis.

The BIA decided to take this project because of a lack of an organization to formally conduct the study in the way it should be. Another reason was that Buddhadasa (Nguam Indapanno) had seen and given importance to the study of the history and archaeological finds related to Buddhism in Chaiya district, Suratthani province. He was even appointed by the Department of Fine Arts to be the Founding Director of Chaiya National Museum at Wat Phra Borommathat Chaiya (in B. E. 1950). Buddhadasa wrote a book titled "Archaeology Around Ao Ban Don" (in B. E. 1950) in order to show that there was evidence that our ancestors had realized the value of and strongly supported Buddhism until it reached its peak in the Srivijaya period. These factors strengthened the faith and effort in the learning, the practice, and the spread of Buddhism as started by our ancestors. The study of Suvarnabhumi by the Buddhadasa Indapanno Archive therefore was conducted to follow the example of Buddhadasa (Nguam Indapanno) himself.

We very much hope that the study and this report, completed by the strong dedication of Dr. Anna Bennett, will be considered in the field of archaeology as one of the first pieces of scientific study on ancient gold in Southeast Asia. Given the ancient finds, specific location, and the quantity which is enough to confirm its source, we hope that the study will be beneficial to further investigation and will eventually lead to more findings about Suvarnabhumi, an area which is closely related to the establishment of

Buddhism in Thailand as well as Southeast Asia. The BIA counts this project as one of the pieces of work conducted on the occasion of worshipping 111 years of Buddhadasa (Nguam Indapanno) on 26 May 2017. We would like to express our heartfelt thanks to all the organizations and people involved including the River Books in co-publishing, a few mentioned here and so many more for their kindness and support on this study. Our special thanks to Dr. Anna Bennett who volunteered to take on this study. We would like to thank Miss Darunee Wiriyaiamphigoon, an officer at DASTA U Thong, and Mr. Pairoj Singbun, the Manager of SuthiRatana Foundation, for his tireless effort providing excellent coordination as well as co-designing this book with Dr. Anna Bennett.

Buddhadasa Indapanno Archives
27 May 2016

GOLD AND EARLY SOUTHEAST ASIA
BY JOHN GUY

Gold in early Southeast Asia is not universally abundant. Large tracts of the region, including most of lowland Southeast Asia, and Java for example, have minimal natural supplies. Fortunately the innumerable streams that flow from the interior highlands to the coasts of Sumatra, Borneo and Vietnam have proved rich sources of alluvial gold since antiquity. Speaking of the river Indus, which begins life in the western Himalayas and winds its way down to Arabian Sea in Pakistan, the ancient Indian text, the *Rgveda*, likely dating to the second millennium BCE, says: *This river with his lucid flow attracts you more than all the streams...Sindhu [Indus] with his path of gold.*[1] The authors of the *Rgveda* could have been writing of the innumerable rivers of Southeast Asia which have long supplied nuggets of gold, panned from its river beds, for fashioning into objects of adornment, both sacred and profane. Since the beginnings of the history of metallurgy in Southeast Asia, gold has been harvested, first gathered as particles from streams and other alluvial sources, and then extracted from mined ore.

The antiquity of gold extraction and working in central Thailand, the concern of this pioneering publication, extends back to proto-historic times. Precious metals, together with such base metals such copper and tin, were important items of both regional and long distance trade, as suggested by studies which explore the possibility of tin from peninsular Southeast Asia being traded to the Indian subcontinent as a key ingredient in the casting of 'silvered bronzes' in the early centuries CE.[2] Recent findings in the peninsular region point to the early reciprocity of trade, with such early north Indian artefacts as a Shunga era (2nd - 1st century BCE) ring stone with raised décor (fig. 2.35-37), likely a jeweller's mould, being found, and a gold seal in Brahmi script (fig. 1.65). These finds are revolutionizing our understanding of the sophistication, complexity and antiquity of this exchange system.[3]

Other objects serve to bring a human dimension to our understanding: a goldsmith's touch stone found at Krabi in peninsular Thailand, that we can identify, thanks to its Tamil Brahmi inscription, as the personal tool of a master goldsmith of the third century from south India (fig. 2.18). This remarkable find bears witness to an early Indian presence in the region, not only sourcing gold, but also processing, refining and likely fashioning it. On the basis of its inscription, the touchstone can be identified as being the personal property of a Tamil-speaking goldsmith of the 3rd century CE, identified as *Perumpatan*.[4] Goldsmiths such as this are unlikely to have operated independently, but rather would have been members of an Indian merchant guild, such as the Manigramam or the *ainiurruvar*, both of which are known to have been active in Southeast Asia. Goldsmith's guilds were an important part of these merchant consortiums which supported Indian trading activities in Southeast Asia and beyond.[5]

Yet none of this should be surprizing. Indian texts of the early centuries BCE reference India's sea trade with *Suvanabhumi* (Golden Land) and *Suvandwipa* (Golden Island) - likely approximating to mainland and insular Southeast Asia - as a metaphor for numerous allegorical tales of hardship, adventure and redemption. Hindu, Buddhist and Jain texts all contain references to Indian merchants venturing on the dangerous voyage to these distant lands to secure gold. The activities of Indian merchants may well have been the catalyst that first stimulated the commercial scale sourcing of alluvial gold from the rivers of Sumatra and the Malay peninsula. A number of inscriptional references to master mariners (*mahanavika*), better approximating 'sea-captain', have been found in both India and Southeast Asia, including the recent discovery in Ranong province, southern Thailand, of a gold personal seal (figs. 1.66, 67).[6]

Gold played a significant role in Southeast Asia's Iron Age (500 BCE - 500 CE). The association of gold with bodily adornment and funerary rites of passage is made clear by their repeated excavation in association with metal artefacts and skeletal remains.[7] The degree to which gold was an elite material in these early societies in unclear – when the Spanish first recorded contact with clan leaders of Samar in the southern Philippines in 1543, they marvelled at the "collars of gold" worn by the *datu's* (chief's) oarsmen, and the fortune adorning him.[8] When naturally occurring nuggets of gold could be retrieved from river beds, hammered and worked into objects of adornment, or for dressing the dead, or both, its luxury status is unquestionable. Over time, and as greater added value was invested in fabricating this material into high quality objects, so they attracted a social status, appropriate to the owner's position in society. The wearing of gold ornaments came to express social standing and to define marital and clan affiliations, just as in some Southeast Asian societies sumptuary rules restricted the wearing of particular textile designs, imbued with specific symbolism embodying authority understood by the wider social group.

The early urban landscape of mainland Southeast is only beginning to be understood as a complex web of small territorial units ruled by local chieftains that evolved into a series of major cities governed by hereditary clan leaders. In the course of the first millennium CE, these urban centres, known in Tai as *muang* (fig. 1.13), to the Burmese as *main*, the Khmer usually as *pura*, and the Malays as *negari*, came increasingly to display the trappings of Indic culture, expressed in the writing of their spoken languages in Indic scripts, the adoption of Sanskrit for ritual use, and the worship of Brahmanical and Buddhist deities.[9] The centres of urbanization were distinguished by large moats and earthwork walls, doubtless capped with palisades that encompassed substantial areas of defendable urban core and significant population concentrations. One of the earliest, and most important in lower central Thailand, was U Thong, in Suphanburi province. Its origins and evolution as a major urban centre and a polity of importance in first millennium central Thailand is presented in the chapters that follow, along with the archaeological objects which bear witness to this evolution, and signal the connectivity of such *muang* through regional and long distance trade.

This publication by Dr. Anna Bennett has at its centre a scientific study of ancient gold in the life of the urban polity of U Thong. As perhaps the premier city-polity within the Dvāravatī territories along with its sister city, Nakhon Pathom, U Thong displays all the hallmarks of a mid-first millennium city-state build on the twin economic drivers of a rich agrarian base and connectivity via the inland river systems to long distance trade. Prosperity was signalled in a number of ways, and in addition to temple building, water management and the expansion of road systems, the ruling elite felt compelled to display their wealth with highly prized accoutrements. With the Sanskritization (and Brahmanization) of the elite, witnessed in the adoption of Indic titles and religious practices, surely they were not untouched by the Indic attitudes to gold, its powerful symbolism and inherent metaphors. Much of the mythology surrounding gold in mid-first millennium Southeast Asia was undoubtedly part of the Sanskritic culture that was circulating with the presence of Indian Brahmin and their descendants, educated in the *Vedas*. They increasingly assumed positions of influence at the courts of Southeast Asia, as providers of ritual service and purveyors of magic. In the *Vedas*, gold is always auspicious, and mentioned in ritual texts alongside flowers and sweet perfumes as pleasing to the gods. In this vision gold is one of the eight auspicious objects (*astamangala*), revered for its brilliant energy, radiance, and auspiciousness. This is vividly demonstrated in the gold Buddha and *dharmacakra* disk of

U Thong (2.2, 2.8) and the spectacular gold *linga kośa* of Champa.[10] That some gold ornaments in first millennium Southeast Asia were directly inspired by Indian imports is vividly demonstrated by a recent study of ear ornaments in central and eastern Java.[11]

This publication brings a new perspective to the study of ancient gold from U Thong. The author is a trained research metallurgy scientist, and it is these skills that have been brought to bear on the highly significant corpus of early gold artefacts found in and around the moated city, the largest accumulation of such artefacts from any of the ancient *muang* of Thailand. Our understanding of such objects – their alloy composition, their construction and their meaning –are addressed in this pioneering study. From her doctorial fieldwork in Lopburi province in the years 1984 to 1988, and frequent return visits to investigate new finds, she has been scientifically engaged with this region for some 32 years. This study of archaeological gold finds of U Thong is an important contribution to the growing body of work being done in Southeast Asia, building the scientific foundations upon which to erect the framework of an early history of central Thailand and those regions beyond its peripheries.

---

1 Rgveda, VIII, 26.18.

2 Glover, Ian 1990b. *Early Trade between India and Southeast Asia: A Link in the Development of a World Trading system.* Occasional Paper No 16, University of Hull: Centre for South-East Asian Studies. 2nd revised edition.

Glover, Ian and Anna Bennett 2012. The High-Tin Bronzes of Thailand. In *Scientific Research on Ancient Asian Metallurgy: Proceedings of the Fifth Forbes Symposium at the Freer Gallery of Art,* Eds. Paul Jett, Blythe McCarthy, and Janet G. Douglas: 101–14, London: Archetype Publications.

3 Bellina, Bérénice, and Praon Silapanth 2006. Khao Sam Kaeo and the Upper Thai Peninsula: Understanding the Mechnisms of Early Trans-Asiatic Trade and Cultural Exchange. In *Uncovering Southeast Asia's Past Choice of papers from the 10th International Conference of the European Association of Southeast Asian Archaeologists, London 14–17th September 2004,* Eds. Bacus, E.A., Glover, I.C., and Piggott, V.C., Singapore: National University Press: 379–392.

4 Guy 2010, "Tamil Merchants and the Hindu Buddhist Diaspora in Early Southeast Asia," in P-Y Manguin and A. Mani (eds.), *Early Interactions Between South and Southeast Asia: Reflections on Cross-Cultural Exchange.* Singapore: Institute of Southeast Asian Studies/ Delhi, Manohar, 2010: 248-49.

5 Guy, 2010.

6 Bellina, Berenice, 2014. Southeast Asia and the Early Maritime Silk Road. In John Guy, *Lost Kingdoms. Hindu-Buddhist Sculpture of Early Southeast Asia,* The Metropolitan Museum of Art, Yale University Press: 23.

7 See for example:

Higham, Charles 2002. *Early Cultures of Mainland Southeast Asia.* Bangkok: River Books.,

Reinecke, Andreas, Vin Laychour, Seng Soneta 2009. The first Golden Age of Cambodia: Excavation at Prohear. Bonn: German Foreign Office.

8 Bernando de la Torre, cited in John Guy, 2011. Gold in the Philippines. Forms, Meaning and Metamorphosis in F. H. Capistrano-Baker (ed.), *Philippine Ancestral Gold.* Manila: Ayala Museum, Singapore, NUS Press: 181.

9 See Sanskrit Studies Centre 2003 for papers on the presence of Sanskrit in first millennium Southeast Asia. For the sculptural record, see

Krairiksh, Piriya 2012. *The Roots of Thai Art.* Bangkok, River Books.

Guy, John 2014. *Lost Kingdoms: Hindu Buddhist Sculpture of Early Southeast Asia,* Metropolitan Museum of Art, Yale University Press.

10 Guy, John, 2000. The Kosa Masks of Champa: New Evidence. In Wibke Lobo and Stephanie Reimann (eds.), *Southeast Asian Archaeology 1998: Proceedings of the 7th International Conference of the European Association of Southeast Asian Archaeologists, Berlin, 31 August–4 September 1998.* Hull: Centre for South-East Asian Studies: 51–60.,

Guy, John 2014. *Lost Kingdoms: Hindu Buddhist Sculpture of Early Southeast Asia,* Metropolitan Museum of Art, Yale University Press: 167.

11 Guy, John, 2008. Ornaments of Empowerment: The *Kundala-Subang* in Old Javanese Jewellery. *Aziatische Kunst: Feestbundel voor Pauline Scheurleer, Amsterdam,* Rijksmuseum Bulletin, vol. 38, no. 4: 55-61.

DVARAVATI GOLD IN SOUTHEAST ASIAN CULTURAL HISTORY BY JOHN MIKSIC

Southeast Asian civilization experienced a true golden age in the late first millennium CE. In Java, Borobudur and Prambanan were built; in Sumatra, Srivijaya became the renowned centre of a network of communication and trade stretching from Africa to Japan and the western Pacific Ocean. In Cambodia, Champa, and Myanmar, artistic geniuses produced some of the greatest architecture and sculpture ever produced in this aesthetically fertile region. But from what predecessors did these great advances in human creativity descend from? Only recently have scholars begun to probe beneath the great monuments built in Southeast Asia during the ninth through twelfth centuries to examine the forebears of the creators acknowledged as glittering emblems of the heritage of all mankind.

The early centres of Classic Southeast Asian civilisation are not easy to analyse. Their remains are dispersed over wide areas, depicting a patchwork of many small centres which had not yet been woven into larger mandalas under the dominion of cakravartins. Although they were small in scale, their inhabitants were already wealthy enough to own large quantities of ornate jewellery such as imported beads from India and carved stone from Taiwan. They had silver coins, something which the later cultures of Myanmar, Thailand, and Cambodia unaccountably dispensed with. They had so much gold that central and western mainland Southeast Asia including the U Thong area was known to the Indians by a Sanskrit name Suvarnabhumi, the Golden Land.

Because the early Classic sites were widely dispersed and because they have received relatively little attention from scholars and protection from authorities compared to the later monuments, they have suffered disproportionately from looting. They thus experienced a double whammy: they were small to begin with, and possessed relatively modest architectural remains, so that their sophisticated economy and social structure has become particularly difficult to study due to the large-scale systematic theft of the type of wealth which they possessed in abundance: small, easily portable, but extremely valuable artifacts which could have shown us much more about the tastes, foreign connections, and symbolic behaviour of the Protoclassic people of Southeast Asia than we are ever going to know.

The sparse data available show that an archaeological culture closely linked to an ethno-linguistic group called the Mon spread over much of Suvarnabhumi from central and southern Thailand to Cambodia and south Vietnam in the mid-first millennium CE. Although one scholar has argued that the Mon people were not present in Myanmar until the Middle Classic period around the twelfth century,[1] coins and early foundations of buildings made of laterite very closely related to those found as far east as Vietnam have been found in the area of Myanmar linked by passes through the mountains to Thailand. Mon speakers live in that area today. From the Three Pagodas Pass a route further north along the Ayeyarwadi is charted by the discovery of similar coins linked to another shadowy archaeological culture termed Pyu. Although the Pyu culture is separate from the Mon culture, the two had strong links to each other. In addition to coinage, they were both mainly Buddhist in religious affiliation.

The name Dvaravati has been found stamped on a few silver medallions or coins found in Thailand. This is a Sanskrit compound known in classical Indian literature as the name of a very important kingdom. This name has been applied to a group of archaeological sites with similar remains of art and architecture which date from the early part of the first millennium to the tenth century. They were ancestral to later Khmer art in Cambodia.[2]

Previous generations of scholars assumed that this cultural homogeneity implied the existence of political unity, specifically a kingdom called Dvaravati, in central and north-eastern Thailand. Current scholarship is critical of this assumption. The nature of the links, currents, and contents of communication within this entity are a matter of considerable interest to scholars since it is now appreciated that Southeast Asian societies were integrated by very different principles from those in better-known civilizations in Asia and the West. Trade and religion were much more important in cementing relationships than military force. Although we have lost much the better part of the pattern of tangible remains from this culture, scholars are becoming increasingly adept at extracting knowledge with what little has survived.

One of the most imposing sites associated with the Dvaravati culture is U Thong. The site is located at the northern end of the delta in which the Chao Phraya River splits into a number of major and minor distributaries. The site includes an oval moat 1,690x840 meters and earthen embankments within which are remains of brick monuments. Archaeological remains include remnants of plaster coating for the brick buildings, ceramics, iron tools, remnants of metal working such as iron slag, glass beads, and spindle whorls for weaving. Radiocarbon dates for the site indicate occupation from the third century BCE to the seventh century CE.[3] The site shares many similarities with Oc Eo, in the Mekong Delta, which probably formed part of a kingdom known to the Chinese of the third to sixth centuries as Funan. A seventh-century copper plate inscription written in Sanskrit from the seventh century mentions King Harsavarman, grandson of Isanavarman. The French scholar Jean Boisselier suggested that U Thong could have been Funan's capital, though other scholars reject this conclusion.[4] U Thong was a significant site with a long lifespan, but it does not seem to have been politically or culturally part of Funan.

The name U Thong was used for a district in the fourteenth century, when a chief or prince of U Thong, possibly the son of a Chinese merchant born in 1314, according to one version of the Royal Chronicles of Ayutthaya, established a royal centre on an island in the Chao Phraya in 1351. This became the capital of Ayutthaya. Thus U Thong's importance persisted long after the Early Classic period.

Gold has been one of the main temptations which lured looters to the vicinities of mounds of soil and laterite blocks. Dvaravati culture metallurgists were expert in a number of media, including the elaborate bronzes illustrated in this book, as well as gold and iron production.

Southeast Asian archaeologists who deal with the Classic period have tended to specialize in art and writing, but have lacked the ability to combine this expertise with quantitative laboratory research. This is in large part due to traditional educational systems which rigidly separate the arts from the sciences. This unfortunate dichotomy is gradually being bridged. One of the best examples of this trend toward reconciliation and synergy between the two scholarly cultures is seen in this volume. The results of the metallurgical studies contained herein demonstrate clearly how the two approaches to the study of the past complement each other. Metal artisans of the past had to possess expertise in both areas (creative and industrial), and archaeologists who wish to understand their work should have the same combination of skills.

One of the most important examples of the way in which art and science overlap is found in the study of the techniques used to produce the artifacts described in this book. Machines can tell us the percentages of different elements in the artifacts, but only a human brain can reconstruct the procedures which led to the final product. These could be quite complex, as the example of the artifact in Figures 1.61 and 1.62 shows (pages 28-29). The Southeast Asian goldsmiths who appear in early Indian literature were as respected as those in India.

It is strange that very little scientific attention has been devoted to the study of Southeast Asian gold. Southeast Asian goldsmiths were as highly skilled as those anywhere else in the world, but almost all previous studies of these artifacts have been written by people like me, who can only use their eyes to compare the overall shapes and styles of gold work to draw conclusions regarding its age and place of origin. The author of this book is one of a small group of people who possess the necessary technical skills combined with archaeological experience in Southeast Asia to be able to study this dimension of gold objects.

Prohear in southeastern Cambodia was the first site to yield a significant amount of gold in a systematic excavation.[5] Those artifacts date from the late Preclassic and early Protoclassic, thus slightly earlier than the U Thong gold objects. The analysis of their composition has provided significant data about late prehistoric gold working and status in Southeast Asia.

Much recent archaeological field work has been conducted at U Thong. This book presents data on this site previously unpublished in English. The information on the large number of sites in the U Thong district with ancient beads, and their distribution inside and outside the city walls is extremely valuable; very few gold objects are found in normal archaeological excavations. Chance finds make up by far the bulk of discoveries of ancient gold artifacts. The contexts of the finds often are unknown. Without this information, any type of artifact, whether made of gold or common materials, can only yield a small amount of information. The role of technical analysis of gold artifacts is accentuated by the dearth of other types of data which these unprovenanced artifacts can yield. The fact that the study of ancient Southeast Asian gold is still in its infancy is thus very strange, since gold objects often contain large quantities of potential knowledge about ancient societies. Gold objects are small, but were usually worked by the most skilled artisans, and therefore form concentrated bundles of stylistic (and symbolic) as well as technical information. The same techniques used on gold were also applied to the ornamentation and production of other metal items. Study of gold working methods can be useful for specialists studying other types of metal objects.

One of gold's attractions for the archaeologist is the fact that jewellery is very sensitive to stylistic changes. Fashions in jewellery change frequently; in the absence of a method for dating gold directly, seriation by style has the potential to provide a chronology for the age of the object. Seriation however requires either stratigraphic information for some stages of the evolution of a motif or shape, or close association with organic material datable by radiocarbon. Some gold objects in ancient Southeast Asia consist of a layer of gold with a core of tree resin. That material can be dated by radiocarbon. This dating method has yet to be exploited in the study of gold. The data on the contexts of the U Thong gold objects, slim though it may be, is of major importance at this stage in the study of this type of object.

Metallurgical studies could be of great utility in the endeavour to date gold items, and also to distinguish genuine from fake pieces. Despite the obvious benefit of this source of information to museums and private collectors, little research on this subject has been published. Gold is of course a rare element in the earth's crust. Gold's allure has led to a vibrant trade of gold both in the form of ore and finished objects. If individual artifacts could be traced to their source, this would be very useful in reconstructing ancient trade balances and routes. Unfortunately no method to identify the source(s) of gold used to make jewellery has been discovered. There are two reasons for this. One is the fact that it is difficult if not impossible to identify trace elements which could be used to fingerprint gold from specific sources (though Bennett discusses some examples where this has been tried with some success). The second is that gold jewellery is frequently recycled when it goes out of style. As a result, gold from different sources is often mixed together. The study of gold working techniques could make a major contribution to the problem of tracing the movements of ancient gold; it is quite possible that specific techniques were characteristic of specific localized gold working traditions.

As an example, in the 1990s Ursula Franklin, a metallurgist in Toronto, studied a few pieces of the Hunter Thompson collection now in the Yale University Art Gallery. She used a scanning electron microscope to try to identify the solder which she assumed had been used to attach some granules of gold to a larger piece. To her surprise, she discovered that the supposed granules had actually been produced by the lost wax casting method, and were made in one piece with the hoop of which they formed part. It is not known whether this was an unusual variation on the normal production technique used in Java during the Classical period, or the standard procedure. Josef Riederer did analyze the elemental composition of some pieces in the Thompson collection.[6]

The catalogue section of this book illustrates the position of the U Thong gold jewellery tradition within that of Southeast Asia. There are many parallels with artifacts found in Cambodia, Thailand, and Indonesia. The "bird rings" for example were previously known mainly from the Thompson Collection believed to have originated in east Java. The similarity between these and some of the artifacts from U Thong indicates that this shape was once shared between mainland and island Southeast Asia, although the U Thong examples (Fig. 3.76- 3.78) have unique traits. The ear ornaments which can be opened and closed is another type found in several other parts of Southeast Asia.

This book forms an important addition to the small number of technical studies of ancient Southeast Asian gold work. The focus on the techniques of the goldsmiths marks a new and very valuable expansion of our knowledge about this subject. Gold was relatively plentiful in ancient Southeast Asia, and in many times and places it seems to have been possible for people of relatively modest means to afford it. Gold artifacts thus provide a significant source of information about Southeast Asian society in general during the Classic period, not just the elite but the common people as well. As a window into this understudied ancient civilization, gold deserves much more attention from scholars in addition to the collectors who have long recognized the artistic importance of this material. Perhaps this book will stimulate other scholars to apply similar research techniques to other collections so that a large body of data can be compiled and new insights into ancient Southeast Asian can be obtained.

---

1 Michael Aung-Thwin 2005. *The Mists of Rāmañña: The Legend That Was Lower Burma.* University of Hawaii Press: Honolulu

2 Brown, Robert L. (1996) *The Dvaravati Wheels of the Law and the Indianization of South East Asia.* Leiden: E.J. Brill.

3 Loofs[-Wissowa], H.H. (1979) Problems of continuity between the pre-Buddhist and Buddhist periods in Central Thailand, with special reference to U Thong. In R.B. Smith and W. Watson (eds) *Early South East Asia.* New York/Kuala Lumpur: Oxford University Press. Pp. 342-351

4 Bronson, Bennet (1979) The late prehistory and early history of central Thailand with special reference to Chansen. In R.B. Smith and W. Watson (eds) *Early South East Asia.* London: Oxford University. Pp. 315-336

5 Reinecke, A., V. Laychour, and S Sonetra (2009) *The First Golden Age of Cambodia: Excavations at Prohear.* Bonn: Thomas Muster.

6 Riederer, Josef 1994 The goldsmith's techniques: the technological analysis of early gold objects from Java. In W.H. Kal (ed) *Old Javanese Gold* (4th-15th Century): An Archaeometrical Approach. Amsterdam: KITLV. Pp. 46-57.

AUTHOR'S PREFACE

Personal reflection: The importance of science in the study of ancient materials.

This book developed out of an invitation by DASTA, Designated Area for Sustainable Tourism Administration, a Public Organisation which was established in 2003, to hold a workshop in U Thong in the summer of 2015. The Dvaravati gold objects within the collections of the National Museum of U Thong, the National Museum of Bangkok and a private collection which has long been known to the museum and which forms an important part of the small amount of surviving Dvaravati gold were studied. The workshop itself proved very successful and led to the request to produce a book in English which would introduce U Thong and its archaeology to a wider audience and be accompanied by a catalogue of the material itself. Having been told that there would be no restrictions on the number of colour photographs made it an impossible request to refuse and I simply jumped at the opportunity. How many articles have I written trying to describe something that a single photograph could explain so much more succinctly? As a result of the numerous photographs in the present volume I hope this book will find a wider audience than the handful of academics already familiar with the material and that it will facilitate comparison to other material in the future, hopefully stimulating curators and conservators to study the techniques of manufacture of objects in their own collections, thus building up a large enough data base of the variations in materials used in different areas and at different periods of time, of the differences in technology and of the variations in fabrication techniques when producing stylistically very similar objects.

Today, scientific techniques are becoming an accepted part of an object's profile and details concerning methods of manufacture and materials should in my opinion be routinely, rather than exceptionally, part of an object's catalogue entry. Understanding the techniques of manufacture of ancient gold is fascinating for its own sake providing ever new insights into the ancient world. But it also provides archaeologists and art historians with a better understanding of the socio-economic conditions of a given place at any given time. The colour of gold and its unchanging durability have afforded this widely dispersed yet rare metal an unchallenged status in the material world. Wherever it has been found, it has attracted and motivated man and, having both ritual and amuletic significance it has been extensively used for personal adornment. Gold ornaments have always been prestige goods indicating not only rank status and wealth within a community but also used as a means of displaying political and cultural affiliations within a wider geo-political region. From the late centuries BCE gold ore and gold items were traded and exchanged with ever increasing demand along established routes within South, Southeast and East Asia. The growth in trade of these highly prized rare prestige goods accompanied the expansion of the new emerging power structures in this dynamic period of the early Christian Era and would no doubt have fueled the instigation and development of new trade routes, both overland and overseas.

As an archaeological and museum scientist, my interest lies in unraveling the history of the objects left behind by past cultures. By examining these objects we can gain insights into how and where they were made and where the raw materials came from, thus documenting the extensive, complex and often indirect trade routes involved. While working on this U Thong gold project it became much clearer to me to what extent religion and the spread of Hindu/Buddhism over 2000 years ago was accompanied by a transfer of culture. Monasteries which were primarily and strategically located close to trade routes were large consumers of exotic goods thus creating an expanding economic order which connected ancient production and trading centers across the whole of Asia. Traveling pilgrims would have established networks of intellectual exchange thus making Buddhist teachings available within an interconnected sacred landscape through which craftsmen would have traveled bringing new skills and perhaps raw materials, and adapting readily to local tastes and conditions. The archaeological evidence is that both religion and trade and their symbiotic relationship in the early centuries of the Christian era were the primary forces behind the development of the Dvaravati Kingdom.

If, by historical times, we have inscriptions detailing elaborate gold offerings to temples, there is sadly no information concerning the identity, status, organisation or production system of the goldsmiths themselves, then it must be to the objects that we look to for answers to such questions as how did the jeweler procure his gold? For whom was he making the items? What was the extent of state and or religious control? Was there an unregulated private system? What was the goldsmith's status within the society? Was there a guild structure as known in India? Did the goldsmith work in isolation or in a workshop? Were the workshops in residential areas, religious compounds or both? Were there masters and apprentices? What were the range of techniques employed and did they differ sufficiently to allow differentiation between workshops?

The structure of a society and the status and organisation of the gold craftsmen within it would have influenced the techniques of production. In certain societies we suspect that gold was centrally controlled with a direct consequence that the metal composition would have been of a consistent purity and the technique of casting rather than hammering more prevalent, since the excess metal required in the process would have been of little consequence and would simply have been melted down and reused in the next casting. In areas of Southeast Asia where the commissioning of gold items was on an individual basis with patrons supplying their own gold in the form of scrap or ingots this may well have influenced the chosen method of manufacture. Was there perhaps a community of itinerant goldsmiths traveling throughout Asia producing finished items to order? If we can begin to document the directions of trade and technology used, we can begin to determine the status and significance of objects at the time of manufacture thus building a picture of both the cultural and economic conditions.

Ancient jewellery formed part of a symbolic system which would have been especially susceptible to stylistic changes, as fashion in terms of not only style but also in terms of the materials used and the techniques employed would have been strongly influenced by the political alliances which were in favor at a given moment and according to which trading connections were particularly favorable. The study of its manufacturing techniques can thus help us document not only the complexity of ancient trade routes via the movement of the finished objects themselves but it also enables us to investigate the functioning mechanism and structure of the gold industry itself, tracking not only the trade in raw materials but also the transfer of technology which was involved in object production.

Anna Bennett
20th May 2016

ACKNOWLEDGEMENTS

I most gratefully acknowledge the financial support of DASTA, Designated Area for Sustainable Tourism Administration, a Public Organisation which was established in 2012. I would like to thank Dr. Nalikatibhag Sangsnit the Director General, and particularly the recently retired Deputy Director General Mrs. Sirikul Kasivivat and all her staff who supported this project in every way and who worked tirelessly to help me with the logistics of the object examinations and to facilitate the presentation of the material at lectures given at U Thong National Museum and the Siam Society in 2015. I would also like to extend my thanks to the present Deputy Director General, Mr. Taweebhong Wichaidit for his continued interest and support. In particular my personal thanks go to Mr. Prakrong Saichan, the Director of Planning Section, Miss. Darunee Wiriyaiamphigoo, Mr. Jetana Patanachan, Panwadee Mesnukul, Mr. Matee Yamkasorn and Mr. Pasan Vibulrungsun.

It was with enormous pleasure that I revisited U Thong National Museum where 30 years ago I set up an exhibition of the then recently excavated Ban Don Ta Phet material. On this occasion I am very grateful to Miss. Dendao Silapanon, the Director of the U Thong National Museum and her staff who provided unlimited access to the gold objects in the museum.

I would like to thank Mr. Phnombootra Chandrajoti, Director of the Bangkok National Museum who allowed me access to the gold objects from U Thong that are displayed there.

I am most grateful to Ian Glover, the director of Ban Don Ta Phet excavations in West Central Thailand for much advice and access to all the excavated material, Bérénice Bellina and Praon Silapanth, the directors of Khao Sam Kaeo in eastern peninsula Thailand for allowing me access to the material from the site, to Kim Dung Nguyen and Lê Thị Liên for information and for providing photographs concerning Giong Phet, Giong Ca Vo, Go Thap and Da Noi in southern Vietnam, to U Win Muang (Tampawaddy) in Mandalay, to Khain Myitzu of the Department of Archaeology, Dagon University for translating archaeological reports and to the SuthiRatana Foundation in Nakhon Si Thammarat for allowing me complete access to their collections. To Charles Higham for allowing me to use the photograph from Noen-U-Locke; Bob Hudson for the photograph from Halin; Andreas Reinecke for information on Prohear and Giong Ca Vo; Pierre Baptiste and the Guimet Museum for use of photographs Figs 1.3, 3.67-3.69. My thanks to Bunchar Pongpanich, Pairot Singbun, Karunphol Phanich, Poowadon Duangmee and Kunakorn Vanichviroon for taking some of the photographs; to Marine Penhouet whose assistance with the layout has been invaluable.

I cannot express enough thanks to Peter Skilling for his formidable editorial skills and to Ian Glover for so generously agreeing to proof read the text, both who offered many critical suggestions. My thanks also to Brigitte Borell for reading an early version and to David Weldon for so conscientiously proof reading the final one. To Pairot Singbun Manager of SuthiRatana Foundation. I remain deeply indebted as without his patience, technical assistance with the layout, the maps, the photographs and his unwavering good humour this publication would not have been possible.

I recognise and appreciate the work of John Guy and John Miksic and am extremely grateful for their time in writing the introductory essays.

My greatest thanks are to Bunchar Pongpanich of the Buddhadasa Indapanno Archives (BIA), Bangkok for his unfailing energy and enthusiasm in the study and understanding of the archaeology and the origins of Buddhism in Thailand.

To Phuthorn Bhumadhon and Ian Glover who between them have taught me most of what I know about ancient and modern Thailand I will always be profoundly indebted.

CHAPTER 1

AN INTRODUCTION TO UTHONG'S EARLY HERITAGE

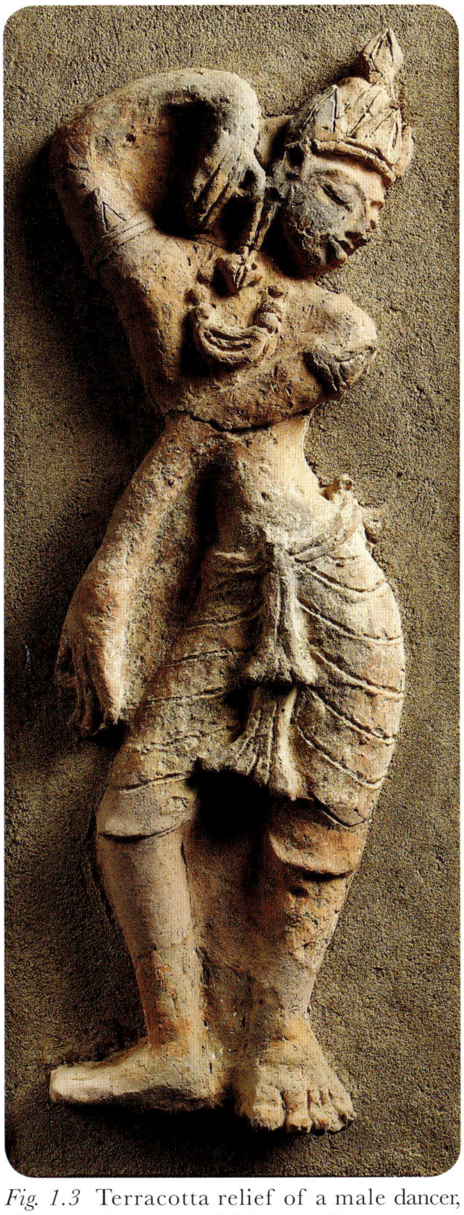

Fig. 1.3 Terracotta relief of a male dancer, National Museum U Thong. Baptiste and Zéphir 2009. Courtesy Guimet Museum, 10/29/2543.

Opposite page
Fig. 1.2 Base of brick monument no. 1 at Muang U Thong, Suphan Buri.

DVARAVATI PERIOD

The city of U Thong in West Central Thailand has long been recognised as an important early centre of Buddhist activity. Archaeological evidence, together with the surviving ancient roads and irrigation canals which still surround the town today, indicate that U Thong was among the earliest urban centres in Southeast Asia. From before the sixth and up to the tenth centuries of the CE, known as the Dvaravati period (Baptiste & Zéphir 2009; Brown 2014, Indrawooth 1999, 2009; Skilling 2003), U Thong would have been populated by townspeople, traders, merchants and craftsmen and served as a pilgrimage centre attracting followers from near and far. AMS carbon 14 analysis of brick and plaster from Watson & Loofs excavation in 1967 by Andrew Barram (2003) and new excavations by San Thaiyanonda (2011) have extended the occupation to well before the sixth CE (Barram & Glover 2008, Glover 2010a, b, Supamas Doungsakun 2015).[1]

Its brick monuments, decorated with resplendent white stucco so characteristic of Dvaravati architecture, would have served as marks of the prestige of this moated city within the wider society.[2] A recently translated 8th century CE Indian copper scroll inscription from Northwestern India describes the magnificence of such monuments (Meltzer and Sander 2006).

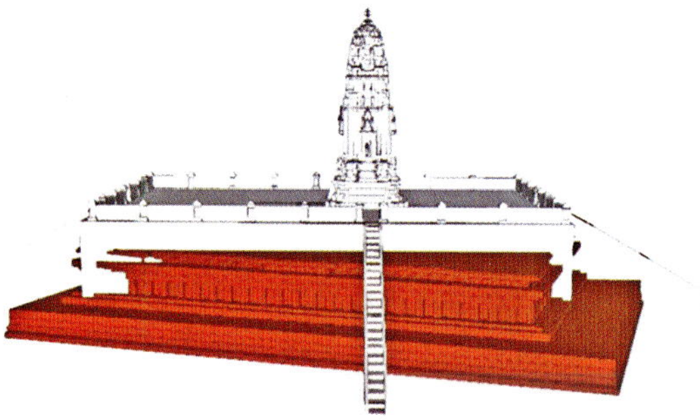

Fig. 1.4 Reconstruction drawing of monument no. 1. Drawing FAD Thailand.

Fig. 1.5 Brick monument no. 1 in a better state of repair than today, photographed in the early 20th century. Courtesy FAD Thailand.

Fig. 1.6 Base of the brick monument no. 1. Photograph taken in 2015.

"Whose stūpas even today light up the earth – mountain like stūpas resembling the colour of white frost, pearl necklaces, white water lilies, crystals and conch shells, raised high by parasols and possessing railings, with flames made up of waving flags, and worshipped by those who are worthy of being honoured by the three worlds –" (Meltzer and Sander 2006:275)

"the place here which is the reason for our birth, which is adorned with stupas resembling a multitute of white autumn clouds .... like lotus ponds, the surface of which has been purified by thousands of sunrays, ...may this great village of the noble ones (aryagrama) be constantly frequented by exalted beings just like heaven" (Meltzer and Sander 2006: 277)

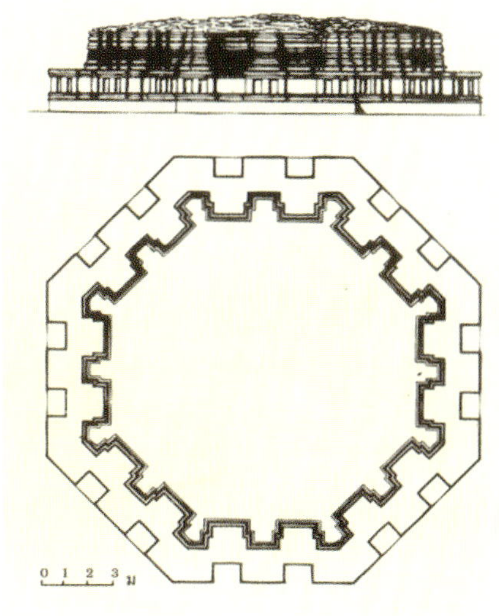

Fig. 1.7 Drawing in Bhumadhon 2015 : 11.5

Fig. 1.8 Monument no.13 at U Thong, 9th century CE. The niches around the base are typical of Dvaravati monuments.

Fig. 1.9 Finial of a monument made of laterite stone which would have originally been covered in stucco.

Fig. 1.10 Stucco fragment found at monument 28, Kulen-Prako style, National Museum U Thong.

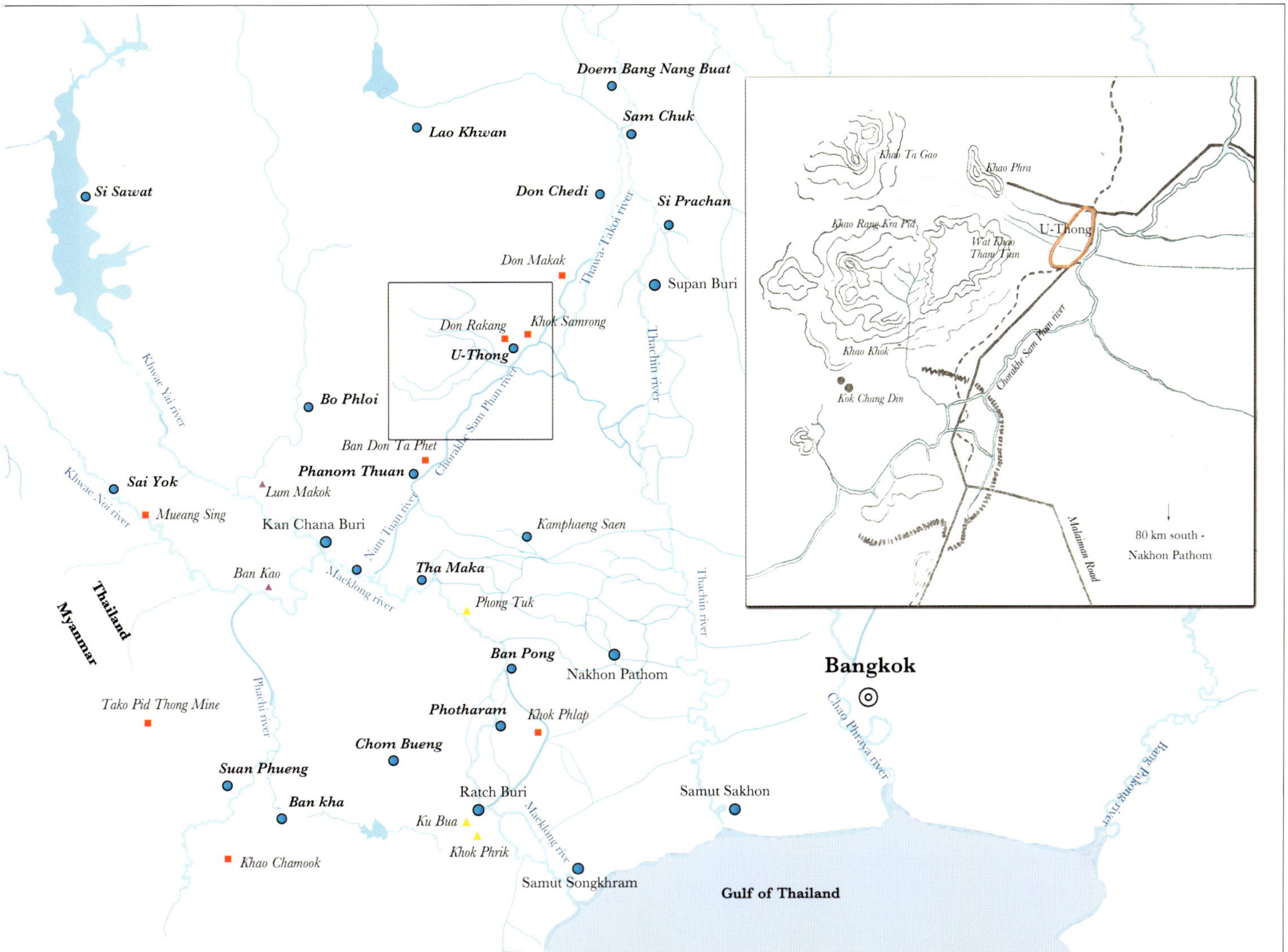

ig. 1.11 Map of U Thong and surrounding area showing the location of the monuments at the top of Khao Rang Kra Pid, Khao Phra and Khao ham Thiam to the north; and the Brahmanical shrines of Kok Chang Din and Khao Khok to the southwest of the city. Drawing adapted by Rot hammapakee in Bhumadhon 2015: 3.4.

Ideally located to function as a central crossroads for trade and commerce, the city, located on the banks of the Chorakhe Sam Phan river within the Maeklong-Thachin River basin, was surrounded by an earthen rampart, a stone wall and a moat.[3] Covering an area of approximately one square kilometre (1.7 km x 0.8 km), with mountains to the north and to the west, the city would have benefited not only from access to the close proximity of forest products and mineral wealth but was also strategically placed in the uplands of the flood plains[4] of the Tha Chin river basin, a distributary to the west of the Chao Phraya river. To the west lay Myanmar, India and Sri Lanka; to the north the communities of the Chao Phraya-Pasak River Basins and China beyond; to the east the Khmer Empire and Champa; and to the south the southern peninsula and the Gulf of Thailand (Fig. 1.1 on inside cover).

"I Sri Harsavarman, grandson of the King, Sri Isanavarman, who has expanded the sphere of his glory, obtained the lion throne by regular succession" (Coedès 1958).

U Thong would have been linked to surrounding smaller settlements via a complex system of waterways[5] and land routes. Over sixty small moated settlements have so far been located and although many of these date to as late as the eleventh century CE others may have been contemporary with the early settlement of U Thong.[6] It was without doubt largely the fertility of the surrounding alluvial soils that allowed the town of U Thong to grow into a major city. Ideal conditions for wet rice cultivation[7] facilitated by the use of iron and animal traction using the water buffalo, would have resulted in a surplus of rice, a prerequisite to supporting the vast labour force and specialisation required to erect and embellish the monuments of ancient U Thong[8] (Figs. 1.4–1.8). Large reservoirs were located to the northwest of the city between Khao Tako Pid Thong (which translates as 'applying gold') and Khao Ta Gao and at least thirty religious buildings have been recorded in the surrounding hills to the west of the city along a 7 km route interspersed on hill tops, at foothills and on the slopes themselves (Fig. 1.11). Many of these Buddhist sites are still in use today (Figs. 1.15–1.24).

There were essentially two types of religious buildings, the stupa which is a reliquary or commemorative structure although it may also have served for religio-political ceremonies, and the vihara, an assembly hall or monastery, many of which were probably constructed in wood and will not have survived. The most renowned stupas are those at the top of Khao Rang Kra Pid, Khao Phra and Khao Tham Thiam to the north which remain sites of worship to the present day. Brahmanical[9] shrines, such as Kok Chang Din and Khao Khok were geographically distinct from the Buddhist sites and were concentrated to the southwest of the city (Fig. 1.13) (Pongpanich & Bhumadhon 2015:101, Supamas Doungsakun 2005, pers. com.).

Together with Nakon Pathom 80 km to the south, which is the largest known Dvaravati site, covering an area of 5.7 square kilometres, U Thong is the earliest and most established moated site within the Chao Phraya valley.[10] A Sanskrit inscription engraved on a copper sheet found within the old city suggests that it may once have been a royal capital.[11]'

Fig 1.12 Ploughing, rice planting and rice fields.

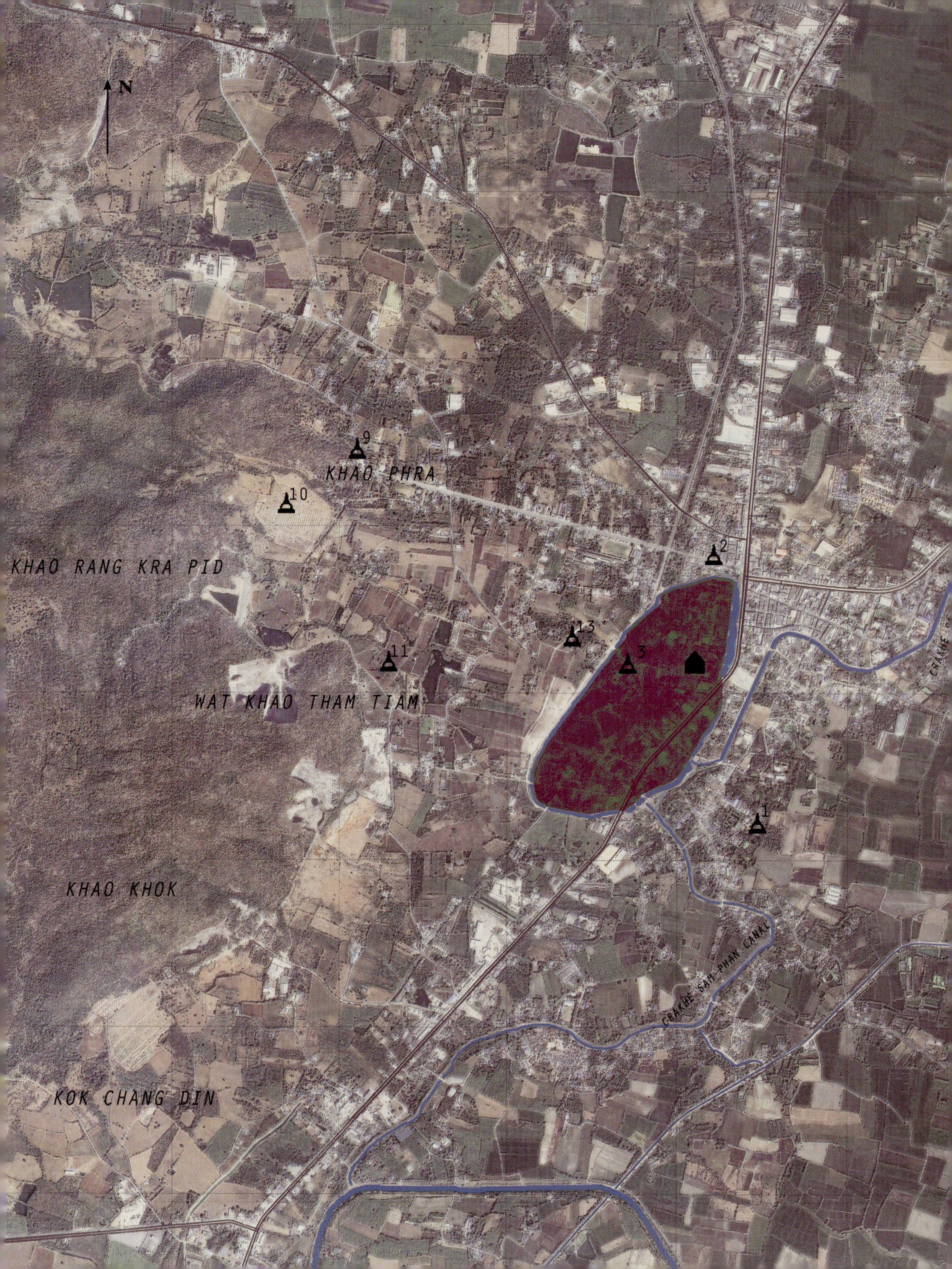
N
9
KHAO PHRA
10
KHAO RANG KRA PID
2
13
11
3
WAT KHAO THAM TIAM
1
KHAO KHOK
CRAKHE SAM PHAN CANAL
KOK CHANG DIN

Fig. 1.14 View of the landscape surrounding U Thong.

Opposite page
Fig. 1.13 Satellite map of U Thong and surrounding area. Courtesy GISTDA, adapted by Rot Dhammapakee and Marine Penhouet.

Figs. 1.15–1.17 Cave sanctuary at Wat Khao Phra with modern Buddhas and archaeological objects.

Figs. 1.18–1.19 Cave sanctuary at Wat Khao Tham Thiam on Khao Rang Kra Pid.

Fig. 1.20 Cave sanctuary still in use today.

Fig. 1.22 Vishnu shrine at Wat Khao Phra.

Fig. 1.21 Monument at Wat Khao Tham Thiam on Khao Rang Kra Pid.

Figs. 1.23–1.24 Brahmanical shrine of Kok Chang Din.

Fig. 1.25 Rising sun coin found at Kok Chang Din. These Pyu silver coins circulated from the 5th to 9th centuries CE, and were probably produced near the Pyu capital of Halin, Myanmar (Moore 2007). Used in trade they have been found at the Funan site of Oc Eo in southern Vietnam and their standardised shapes and weights suggest a degree of central control.
National Museum U Thong.

Fig. 1.26 The finds from Ban Don Ta Phet included a nephrite two-headed animal pendant (*linglingo*) characteristic of Vietnamese Sa Hyunh culture and carnelian and etched beads introduced from India.

Fig. 1.27 Photograph showing Quaritch Wales at U Thong (Quaritch Wales 1937).

The social make up and complexity of U Thong and its surroundings prior to the Dvaravati period are less clear. By definition the protohistoric period lacks substantial historical data; it is without grand monuments and without inscriptions, which appear only in the mid first millennium CE (tenth century Buddhist era BE).

The earliest archaeological descriptions of U Thong are those by George Coedès in *Ars Asiatica* (1928) and by Quaritch Wales (1937) in *Towards Angkor in the Footsteps of the Indian Invader* (Fig. 1.27) where he recorded examples of Brahmanical Siva lingams and a stele of a mitred Visnu. The first archaeological excavations were by Prince Subhadhradisa Disakul in 1959 and the Fine Arts Department of Thailand (FAD) by Somsak Rattanakul in 1961–1966, followed by Boisselier in 1964 (1965, 1966) and by the Thai British archaeological expedition in 1967 by Watson and Loofs (Loofs 1970, 1979; Watson & Loofs 1967) who documented prehistoric pottery beneath the levels containing the sixth or seventh century CE Dvaravati ceramics. Later excavations by Boisselier (1968) and by Quaritch Wales (1969) and more recently the excavations by the Thai and Thai-British teams at the protohistoric cemetery site of Ban DonTa Phet, 25 km to the south in the 1980's (Glover 1990a, Glover, Charoenwongsa, Alvey, & Kammounket 1984) have demonstrated a clear prehistoric background with both economic and cultural links between India and the U Thong area (Figs. 1.26, 1.41–1.52, 1.80, 1.81) and of extensive trading with the communities of Central and southern coastal Vietnam, Northern Vietnam and China beyond.

The city of U Thong was contemporary with the Kingdom of Funan, on the Mekong delta in southern Vietnam, a name we know from Chinese texts which describe it as a powerful political and commercial centre in the third century CE (eighth century of BE). The text describes a king from Funan building a fleet of ships to cross the Gulf of Thailand to conquer more than ten kingdoms (Pryce, Bellina and Bennett 2008).[12] Archaeological excavations in the U Thong area have provided evidence of imported exotic goods which derive from the east, including a particular type of nephrite ear ornament depicting a two headed animal with a bar and a hook for suspension, known as *linglingo* and characteristic of the coastal Sa-Hyunh culture of central and south Vietnam, but the raw material of which has been shown to come only from Taiwan (Figs. 1.26, 1.28, 1.29) (Hung, Iizuka and Bellwood 2006, Hung & Bellwood 2010)[13] and a Dongson style situla from South China or Northern Vietnam (Figs. 1.30, 1.31).

Fig. 1.28 A nephrite two-headed animal pendant known as a *linglingo* ear ornament excavated at Ban Don Ta Phet provides evidence of contact and trading links with Vietnam. Characteristic of the Sa-Huynh Iron Age culture of the central coast of Vietnam, these artefacts were also traded north to the Dong Son sites of Northern Vietnam and east to the Philippines and Taiwan. The jade has been shown to originate only in Taiwan. National Museum, Bangkok. Courtesy Ian Glover.

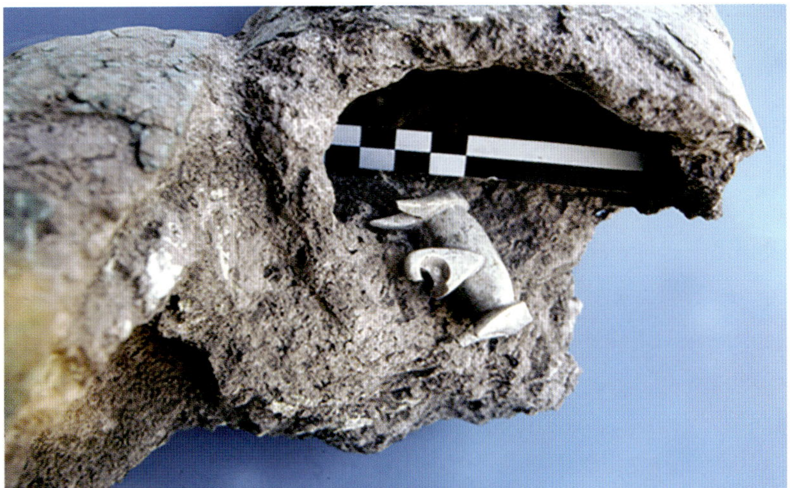

Fig. 1.29 The *linglingo* from Ban Don Ta Phet at the time of excavation found inside a bronze bowl. At the Sa-Huynh site of Giong Ca Vo in southern Vietnam a skull was excavated with this type of ear ornament still *in situ* on the side of the skull. Courtesy Ian Glover.

Fig. 1.30 A wide variety of bronze bowls were excavated at Ban Don Ta Phet, including this situla excavated from burial 56 in 1980/81, which is regarded as a Dong Son import coming from South China or Northern Vietnam and which is so far unique to Thailand. Courtesy Ian Glover.

Ht: 20.5 cm, rim diameter: 21.7 cm.

Cast with thick walls in a high lead, low-tin bronze, with a composition of between 7.2–10.6% tin and 44.5–68% copper with up to 22% lead.

Fig. 1.31 The situla has a ring base with flaring straight sides, two strap handles and a shallow incised fishbone design in a band around the upper section. It was deliberately crushed before burial.

Fig. 1.32 Excavation of Trench A at Ban Don Ta Phet in 1984. Courtesy Ian Glover.

Fig. 1.33 Author lifting a bronze bowl in Trench A in 1984. Courtesy Ian Glover.

Fig. 1.34 Author lifting a bronze bowl and two iron digging sticks.

Fig. 1.35 Co-director Ian Glover cleaning a bronze bowl.

Fig. 1.36 A bronze bowl after conservation.

Fig. 1.37 Unlike most of the bone from the site which no longer survives, a small piece of human bone has been preserved on the side of this bowl due to the high concentration of copper salts.

Fig. 1.38 The site of Ban Don Ta Phet was dated to the 4th century or early 3rd century BCE using grains of rice such as these, which have been preserved on the inside of an excavated pottery sherd.

Fig. 1.39 Carnelian and etched beads in a bronze bowl excavated at Ban Don Ta Phet. Over 3000 beads were excavated at the site. National Museum Bangkok.

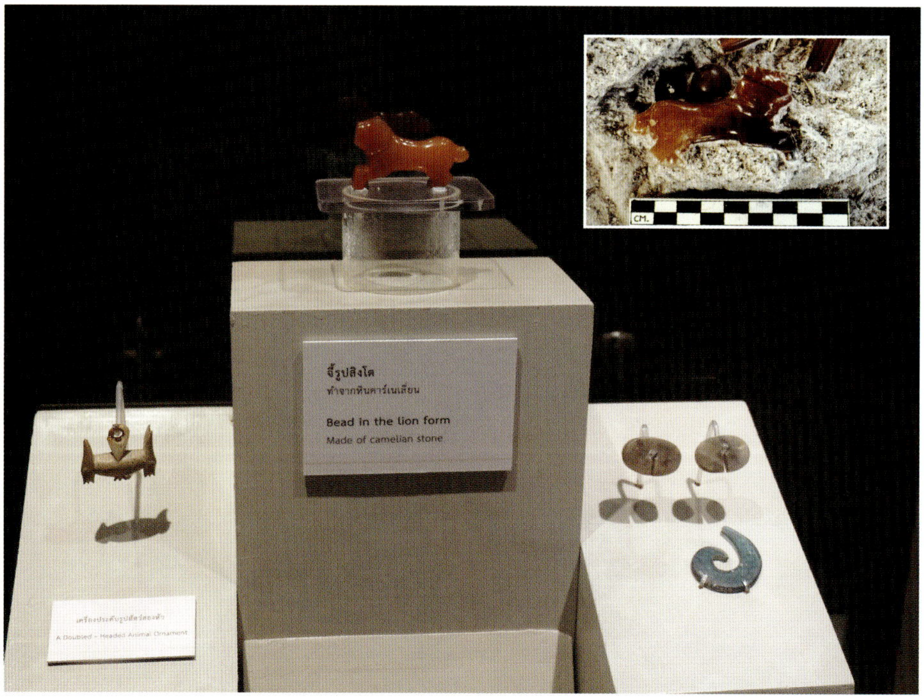

Fig. 1.40 Carnelian lion or tiger excavated within a bronze bowl at Ban Don Ta Phet together with carnelian beads. A similar carnelian tiger was found at Khuan Lukpat in peninsular Thailand and others are reported from the Samon valley in Myanmar where they may possibly have been manufactured. National Museum Bangkok.

Of the three hundred bronzes excavated at the protohistoric cemetery site of Ban Don Ta Phet (C14 dated fourth to late third BCE) many were made of a high-tin bronze (23–28% Sn). This intractable alloy may have been chosen because of its resemblance to yellow gold when freshly polished and because such bowls could be used to serve food at special occasions, without corroding in the manner of a low tin bronze. Cast with thin walls, hot-worked, quenched and annealed to varying degrees, some of the bowls were decorated with fine incised decoration below the rims and a few included scenes of people, houses, horses, cattle and buffaloes (Figs. 1.41, 1.42) which are clearly Indian in style. These bowls are almost identical to those found together with tin ingots at the tin mining sites at Khao Jamook in Chombeung District, Ratcha Buri province, 120 km southwest of U Thong and close to the Myanmar border (Figs. 1.44, 1.45) (Bennett and Glover 1992; Glover and Bennett 2012); to finds from Ban Ta Po, 7 km from Pasat Meung Sing and also close to the Myanmar border (visited by Bennett 2016) and to three complete and one broken bowl found at Khao Sam Kaeo, a coastal settlement and production site in Chumphon province on the southeast coast of the Thai-Malay peninsular, which is contemporary or slightly later than Ban Don Ta Phet (Figs. 1.46–1.51). These high tin bowls are not dissimilar to those found at the early Buddhist settlement of Taxila, within the Ghandaran Kingdom in the Indus valley in present day Pakistan and which are dated to between 5th BCE and 2nd CE (Bennett and Glover 1992, Glover and Bennett 2012, Glover and Shahnaj Husne Jahan 2014). India is tin poor and these bowls are thought to have been produced in India using tin imported from Western Thailand with examples of the finished product being traded back to the Thailand along the silk roads. Interestingly excavations at Tilpi a second to first century BCE metal manufacturing site in the coastal district of West Bengal have produced ingots of high tin bronze found in association with crucible fragments which is the first recording of high tin bronze manufacture in ancient South or Southeast Asia (Datta, Chattopadhyay and Ray 2007).

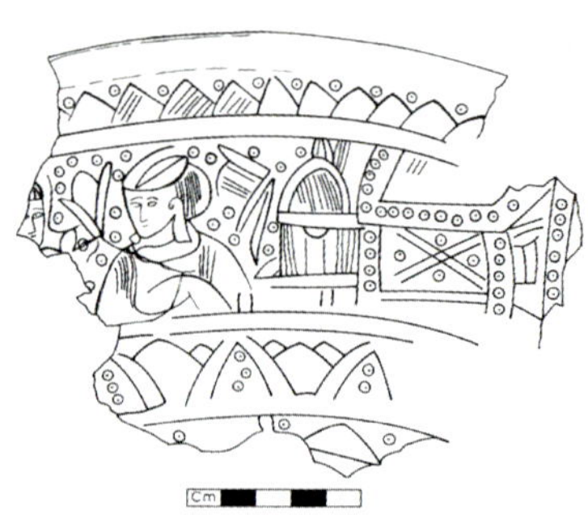

Surface x-ray fluorescence analysis:

Cu: 79.7%
Sn: 20.3%

Figs. 1.41–1.42 High tin bronze bowl excavated at the protohistoric cemetery site of Ban Don Ta Phet, 25 km south of U Thong city, dated to the fourth or late third centuries BCE. National Museum Bangkok. (Glover and Bennett 2012).

Fig. 1.44 Bronze bowl fragment found together with other similar bowl fragments and tin ingots at the tin mining sites at Khao Jamook, Chombeung District, Ratcha Buri province, 120 km southwest of UThong and close to the Myanmar border.

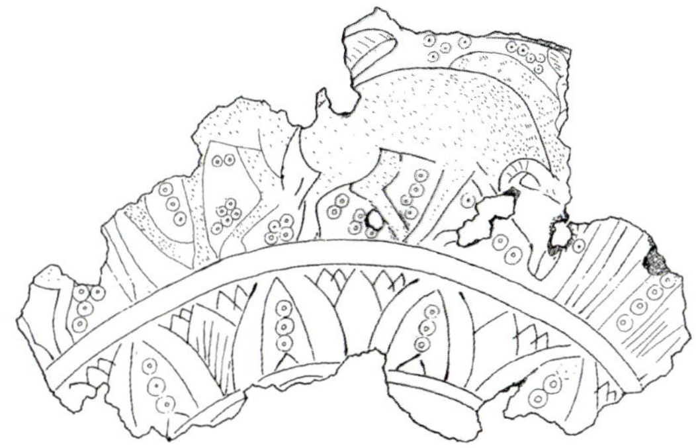

Fig. 1.45 Line drawing of a similar decorated bronze bowl from the same site showing a grazing animal above an open lotus flower at the base of the bowl. (Bennett and Glover 1992, Glover and Bennett 2012). National Museum, Ratcha Buri.

Fig. 1.46 Bowl found at Khao Sam Kaeo on the southeast coast of the peninsula (Glover and Shahnaj Husne Jahan 2014), SuthiRatana Foundation, Bangkok, KSK 525.

Fig. 1.47 Drawing courtesy of Shahnaj Husne Jahan and Kwanpoom Wilaival.

Figs. 1.48, 1.49 Similar high tin bronze bowl found at Khao Sam Kaeo. SuthiRatana Foundation, Bangkok, KSK528. Drawing by Nguan Tretappratina.

	outside	outside	inside
Cu:	47.10%	45.29%	41.61%
Sn:	22.01%	32.06%	29.13%
Fe:	29.77%	21.17%	26.99%
As:	0.62%	0.68%	0.59%
Pb:	nd	nd	nd
Ni:	nd	nd	nd

Fig. 1.50 KSK 528 Surface x-ray fluorescence analysis.

Figs. 1.51–1.52 A third high tin bronze decorated bowl found at Khao Sam Kaeo, SuthiRatana Foundation, Bangkok, KSK554.

	outside, bare metal	outside, bare metal	inside	inside	outside with crust	outside with crust
Cu:	64.13%	60.95%	52.88 %	53.01%	47.75%	46.47%
Sn:	28.23%	28.72%	21.81%	23.83%	33.14%	34.27%
Fe:	6.38%	9.02%	24.20 %	22.36%	18.04%	18.24%
As:	0.33%	0.35%	0.38 %	0.31%	0.38%	0.38%
Pb:	0.13%	0.15%	0.1 %	0.1%	nd	nd
Ni:	0.29%	0.1%	nd	nd	nd	nd

Fig. 1.53 KSK 554 Surface x-ray fluorescence analysis.

SEA TRADE

Archaeological evidence demonstrates that during the late first millennium BCE and the first half of the 1st millennium CE, well before the advent of Brahmanical and Buddhist civilisations, U Thong and the surrounding communities were part of a sophisticated and stratified society that was already trading directly or indirectly with India and China and had at least some contact with the Mediterranean world (Fig. 1.54) (Bellina and Glover 2004; Borell, Bellina and Chaisuwan 2014, Glover 1990b, 1996 a, b, 2010a, Glover and Bellina 2011, Ray 1994, 2014). Ships sailed back and forth across the Gulf of Thailand and the South China Sea in a system of interconnected trade routes. Caravans travelled by land to and from the Andaman Coast near Dawei, across lower Myanmar and the peninsula and up to Kan Chana Buri and the U Thong area using mountain passes and river systems.

The Isthmus of Kra, which is the narrowest part of the peninsula, would have served as a trans-penninsular land crossing connecting the Gulf of Thailand and the Bay of Bengal and its use in the protohistoric and early historic periods is supported by the archaeological record and ancient Chinese texts. The annals of the Western Han dynasty describe a sea voyage, which took place at the end of the first[1] millennium BCE between the southern Chinese ports in the Gulf of Tonkin to a place called Huangzhi, which is thought to be Kanchipurum in Southern India. The text describes a land crossing of ten days, which is thought to be that of the Isthmus of Kra (Wang 1958: 19–20).

The scale of the sea trade in the early historic period is clearly illustrated by the tenth century text Kathakosa (932 CE) which mentions a voyage with five hundred ships (Dube 2003 referring to Majumdar 1936) and a further indication of the importance of this trade comes from Indian coinage of this period which is stamped, with the picture of ships. Three bronze coins with a double masted ship on one side and a humped bull on the other have been found at Khuan Luk Pad in the southern peninsula, one is in the local museum (Indrawooth 2004: 6.5) and two are in the SuthiRatana Foundation (Fig. 1.54). A clay impression of a fourth–fifth century CE Indian seal depicting an oceangoing vessel typical of the first millennium CE with stitched plank construction with a single mast, lantern sail and lateral stern rudder boat was found in Nakon Pathom (Fig. 1.55).

Fig. 1.54 One of two bronze coins with a double masted ship on the reverse and a humped bull on the obverse found at Khun Luk Pad, southern Thailand. SuthiRatana Foundation, Bangkok, KLP399.

Fig. 1.55 A baked clay impression of a fourth–fifth century CE Indian seal depicting an oceangoing vessel typical of the first millennium CE found in Nakon Pathom, ht: 5 cm w: 4.5 cm, diam. 3 cm. National Museum, Bangkok, 2309.

ROMAN COINS AND PENDANTS

Other imported objects found in the U Thong area include the only Roman coin reported from Thailand,[14] a copper alloy issue of Emperor Victorinus (269–271CE) (Fig. 1.57, 1.58);[15] a gold imitation coin worn as a pendant (Fig. 1.59–1.62), and a Byzantine oil lamp (Fig. 1.56) found at Pong Tuek, Kan Chana Buri province (Borell 2008a, b, 2014, forthcoming). Roman coins would have been traded by travelling Indian merchants and although the presence of Western traders in Southeast Asia by the late second to early third centuries CE is recorded in Chinese accounts, these finds represent regional imports from India rather than direct contact with the Mediterranean world.

Figs. 1.57–1.58 The only Roman coin reported from Thailand is a copper alloy coin of the Emperor Victorinus (269–271CE) diam. 20 mm. National Museum, U Thong (306/2509).
© 2016 U Thong National Museum

Fig. 1.56 A large Byzantine oil lamp found at Pong Tuek, Kan Chana Buri. National Museum Bangkok.

Figs. 1.59–1.60 A gold imitation coin worn as a pendant.

The image on this gold imitation coin is not identifiable, not as the result of wear or damage but rather of the manufacturing process. The detail has not been well reproduced: while the front of the pendant depicts a human head and bust facing right, the surrounding circle of short vertical strokes and bosses in relief only simulate the lettering on a Roman coin. The reverse of the pendant is the sunken image of the front suggesting that the pendant was manufactured by hammering into a negative die. However, there are no hammering marks on the gold surface but rather the texture of cast metal. It is possible that the pendant was made from a wax model, made in a stone mould which was then invested and cast using the lost wax casting process. The custom of wearing Roman coins or their imitations is known from Southern India and the idea is presumed to have transferred from there by merchants and traders. Although such pendants may have been imported from India, evidence that at least some of these objects were locally produced comes from a gold coin pendant which was cast in a bivalve mould and which was found together with half of a bivalve mould at Kuan Luk Pat, also called Klong Thom on the west coast of the Thai Malay peninsula. Other examples of coin imitation gold pendants have been found at the ancient port site of Oc Eo in the Mekong delta in southern Vietnam (Borrell 2014). These objects illustrate the far- reaching trade links at this time.

Figs. 1.61–1.62 Reverse of pendant.

Weight: 1.06 g

Ht: 18.02 mm

Width: 18.92 mm (which corresponds to that a roman aureus)

Elemental composition:

Obverse: 79.19% gold, 20.2% silver, 0.05% copper, 0.5% tin

Reverse: 75.3% gold, 24.16% silver, 0.07% copper, 0.35% tin

Manufacture: hammered into a negative die or cast using the lost wax casting process. An extension at the top of the coin, now broken off, would simply have been folded over to form a suspension loop.

Condition: coin complete but with attachment missing, some indentations

Evidence of use: evidence of wear

Find location: found in U Thong as a chance find and bought by the museum in 2006 for 15,000 baht from Mrs Sunee Rankrung, 1706 Tambon sub-district, U Thong

Present location: National Museum U Thong (10/1/2549)

SUVARNABHUMI, LAND OF GOLD

A name for Thailand is Laem Thong, which translates as 'golden peninsula' and the word U Thong itself is translated as golden cradle. Evidence suggests that Southeast Asian gold ores were a stimulating factor in developing early contacts with India and China. Historical sources inform us that the Chinese were impressed by the abundant quantities of gold on the peninsula. Chinese emissaries in the Jin dynasty (265 CE–419 CE) refer to the pre-Angkor kingdom of Funan as having expanded its sphere of influence to encompass those parts of the Malay Peninsula with gold deposits, suggesting that gold was readily available if not locally produced.

Fig. 1.63 Gold recovered from early sites in southern Thailand. SuthiRatana Foundation, Bangkok.

Gold ore is fairly widely, though irregularly, distributed throughout Southeast Asia in the igneous and metamorphic hard-rock deposits and in sedimentary placer deposits. The Southeast Asian mainland, including lower Myanmar and the Thai Malay Peninsula region was known to the Indian merchants of the 1st millennium BCE as *Suvarnabhumi*: 'Land of Gold' and *Suvarnadvipa*: 'Islands of Gold' with is thought to refer to the Indonesian Archipelago including Sumatra. Buddhaswami's fifth-century Sanskrit text Brhatkatha-Slokasamgraha relates the story of merchants who travelled to Suvarnabhumi by sea. Having crossed the "unfathomable" sea, they arrived at a coast and embarked on a long voyage on foot, travelling past the forested foothills of high mountains, which they then crossed, finally reaching a forest and a shallow river rich in gold sands (Dube 2003: 6).

That gold first appears in the archaeological record in 400 BCE at about the same time as iron, semiprecious stone polishing and glass working, suggests that the techniques of extraction and working were introduced to Southeast Asia via Indian and or Chinese merchants seeking gold (Pryce,Bellina and Bennett 2008, Bennett 2010, 2015a).

In his Geography (1.13–14),[16] Ptolemy provides descriptions of the peninsula which he calls Chryse Chersonesos—golden peninsula. Sanskrit synonyms for gold such as Kanaka, Hema and Suvarna, have been used to name rivers and mountains containing either alluvial or vein deposits of gold and the words 'gold' and 'golden' are often associated with place names throughout the region. The Ramayana mentions Sugriva sending his envoys to Hiranyanabha[17] Mountain to the east, i.e. in the direction of Southeast Asia, which was known to be rich in precious metals, in search of Rama's wife Sita.

An eighth-century Indian text known as the Samaraiccakaha, describes a sea voyage to Suvarnadvipa and the making of bricks from the gold rich sands, which they inscribed with the name dharana and then baked (Dube 2003: 6). The sintering of such gold rich sands by mixing the sand with water, and shaping it into bricks may have afforded early gold explorers a relatively easy method of transporting the raw material. Upon return it could then be carefully separated from its sand matrix in the more suitable environment.

Fig. 1.64 Scrap gold from early sites in southern Thailand. SuthiRatana Foundation, Bangkok.

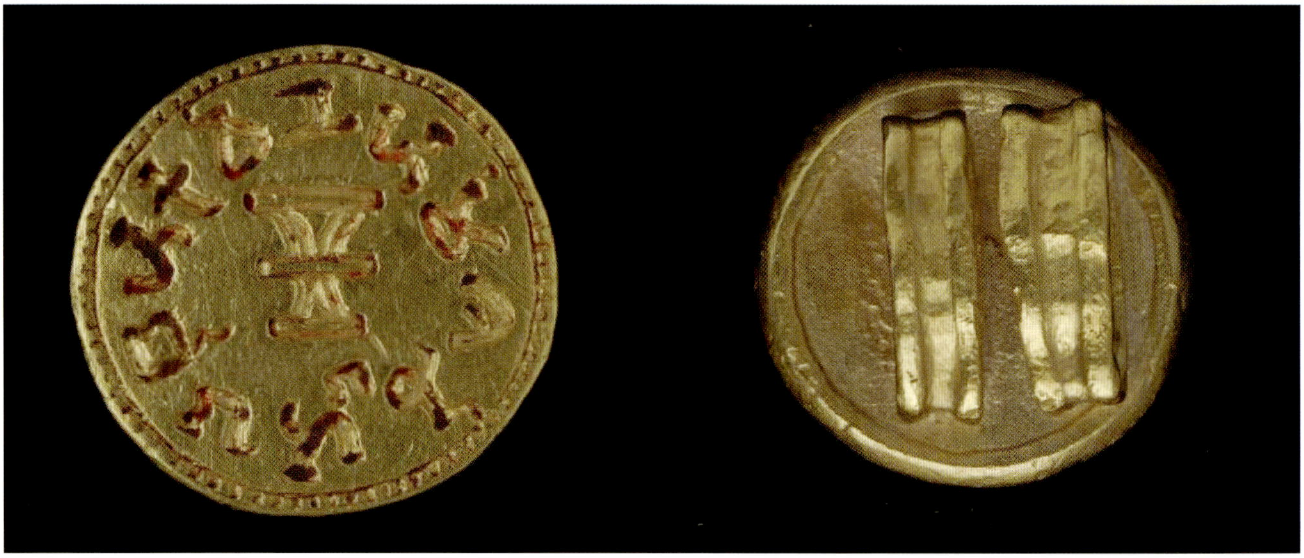

Figs. 1.65, 1.66 Gold recovered from early sites in southern Thailand, including a first or second century CE gold seal bearing the Brahmi inscription *brahaspatiśarmasa nāvika*, 'of the mariner Brahaspati', found at Bang Kluay Nok in Ranong on the western coast of the central peninsula. SuthiRatana Foundation, Bangkok, BKN068

Fig 1.67 Details of the inscription. These photographs are reversed to allow ease of reading.

A first or second century CE gold seal (Figs. 1.66, 1.67) bearing the Brahmi inscription *brahaspatiśarmasa nāvika,* translated by Skilling as 'of the mariner Brahaspati Navika', was found at Bang Kluai Nok in Ranong on the western coast of the central peninsula (Pongpanich 2009, Bellina et al. 2014; Skilling 2015). The second early reference to a mariner (*nāvika*) to be found in Southeast Asia, it has the name Brahaspati engraved into the seal surrounding a *bhaddapitha*, or auspicious seat or throne (Skilling 2015: 63–77). An attachment soldered onto the reverse would have allowed the seal to be secured (Fig. 1.70), and the extensive wear and overlapping scratches visible on the surface indicate that the seal was in circulation for a considerable period before being lost (Fig. 1.68, 1.69). The same site produced Eastern Han mirror fragments and very large quantities of stone and glass beads, seals and intaglios (Bellina et al. 2014).

While it is abundantly clear that there was an extensive trade with both India and China in the early historic periods, the surviving inscriptions, texts, and early travel writings provide very little evidence concerning the organization of the gold supplies. The fifth century Chinese text "History of Southern Ch'i" describes the inhabitants of Funan as having gold, silver, and silks, but there is no indication as to where the gold was sourced "The inhabitants of Funan make rings and bracelets of gold and plates of silver". Zhou Daguan (Chou Ta-Kuan), a Chinese envoy who visited the Khmer complex of Angkor during 1295–96 CE, included in his "Notes on the Customs of Cambodia" descriptions of the Khmer king wearing gold diadems, bracelets, anklets, and rings; his horses decorated with gold; elephant tusks covered in gold; gold parasol handles; and various items of gold jewellery. Unfortunately there is no indication in his accounts of the royal court whether the gold had been exploited locally or gifted as finished articles.[18]

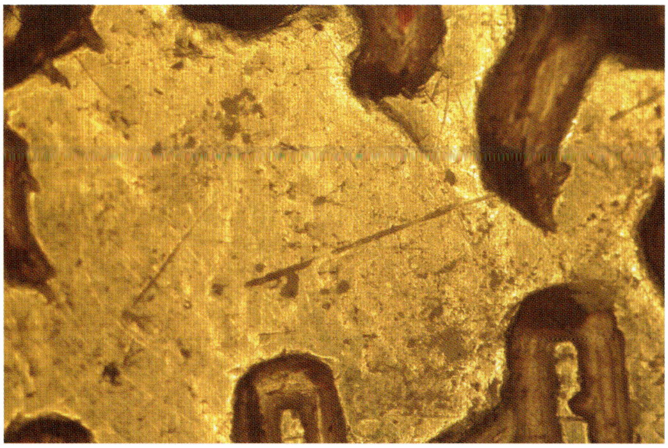

Figs. 1.68–1.69 Photomicrographs showing the extensive wear and overlapping scratches visible on the gold surface. These clearly indicate that the seal was in circulation for a considerable period before being lost.

Fig. 1.70 Reverse of the seal showing the soldered attachment.

COPPER PRODUCTION IN PROTOHISTORIC CENTRAL THAILAND

Fig. 1.71 Dressing stone from Non Mak Kla, Khao Wong Prachan Valley, Central Thailand.

Copper production only 130 km northeast of U Thong in the Wong Pra Chan Valley, was undertaken during the mid second to the end of the first millennium BCE on a large scale at both Non Pawai, Non Mak La and the slightly later site of Nil Kham Haeng (Bennett 1988 a, b, 1989 a, b; Natapintu 1988; Piggot, Weiss, and Natapintu 1997; Piggot and Ciarla 2007) (Figs. 1.71, 1.73). These sites, together with the ancient copper mines in Laos which have been carbon dated to 200 BCE–300 CE (Tucci, Sayavongkhamdy, Chang and Souksavatdy 2014) are among the largest copper production sites known in Asia. All stages of the production process from mining to ore preparation to smelting to casting ingots are attested. There is, however, no evidence of any bronze object manufacturing in the Wong Prachan Valley and the only objects produced at the site were a number of arsenical copper spears, arrows and axes found in graves associated with the site (Fig. 1.73) (Bennett 1989). This suggests that the copper ingots were traded out to other communities who had supplies of tin and perhaps a knowledge of bronze manufacture. The sulphidic copper ore which was being used was smelted in bowl-shaped crucible furnaces dug into the ground with clay lined chimneys to promote an updraft. Copper production was on a vast scale but it appears to have been exclusively organized on a community level with habitation and cemetery sites interspersed within the smelting sites. These were small decentralized production units operating on a seasonal basis[19] and there is no evidence of any specialisation or central organisation (White & Pigott, 1996).

Fig. 1.72 Moulds for casting copper ingots from Non Pawai, Khao Wong Prachan Valley, Central Thailand (Bennett 1989b).

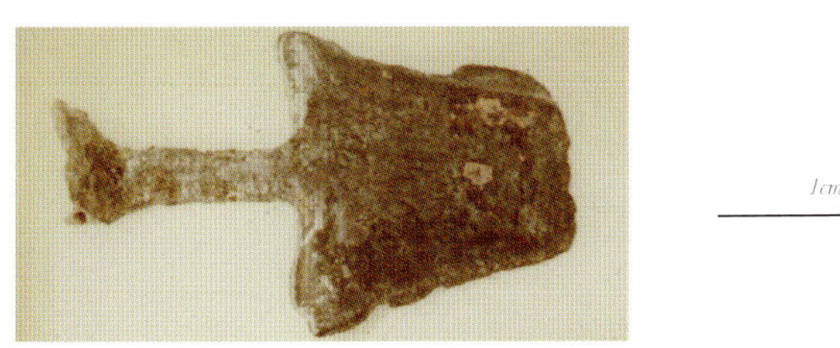

Fig. 1.73 Arsenical copper arrow head from Non Mak Kla, Khao Wong Prachan Valley, Central Thailand (Bennett 1989b).

The superior technical properties of iron for making agricultural tools and weapons would have placed demands on the forces of supply to obtain these appropriate implements. It is true that iron exists as an impurity in copper ores and that iron oxide was used as a primary fluxing agent in copper smelting, so that smelters would have at least been aware of iron rich by-products before iron metal was intentionally smelted (Piggot 1982:21). But iron tools and weapons appear suddenly about the mid first millennium BCE[xxii] (Bennett 2013a, b) at about the same time as gold, semiprecious stone polishing and glass working. This suggests that the technology of iron production may have been imported from South Asia, where it appears at about 1200 BCE in the Northwest of India after which it spreads throughout the subcontinent over the next few hundred years. The shapes of many of the artefacts from the UThong iron age are similar to those found in South Asia and Myanmar (Fig. 1.74–1.78), although the billhooks appear to be exclusive to the Southeast Asian mainland (Bennett 1982, 2015b) (Figs. 1.78, 1.79). There is of course no reason not to suppose that once the iron smelting technology was introduced, local production would have rapidly followed.

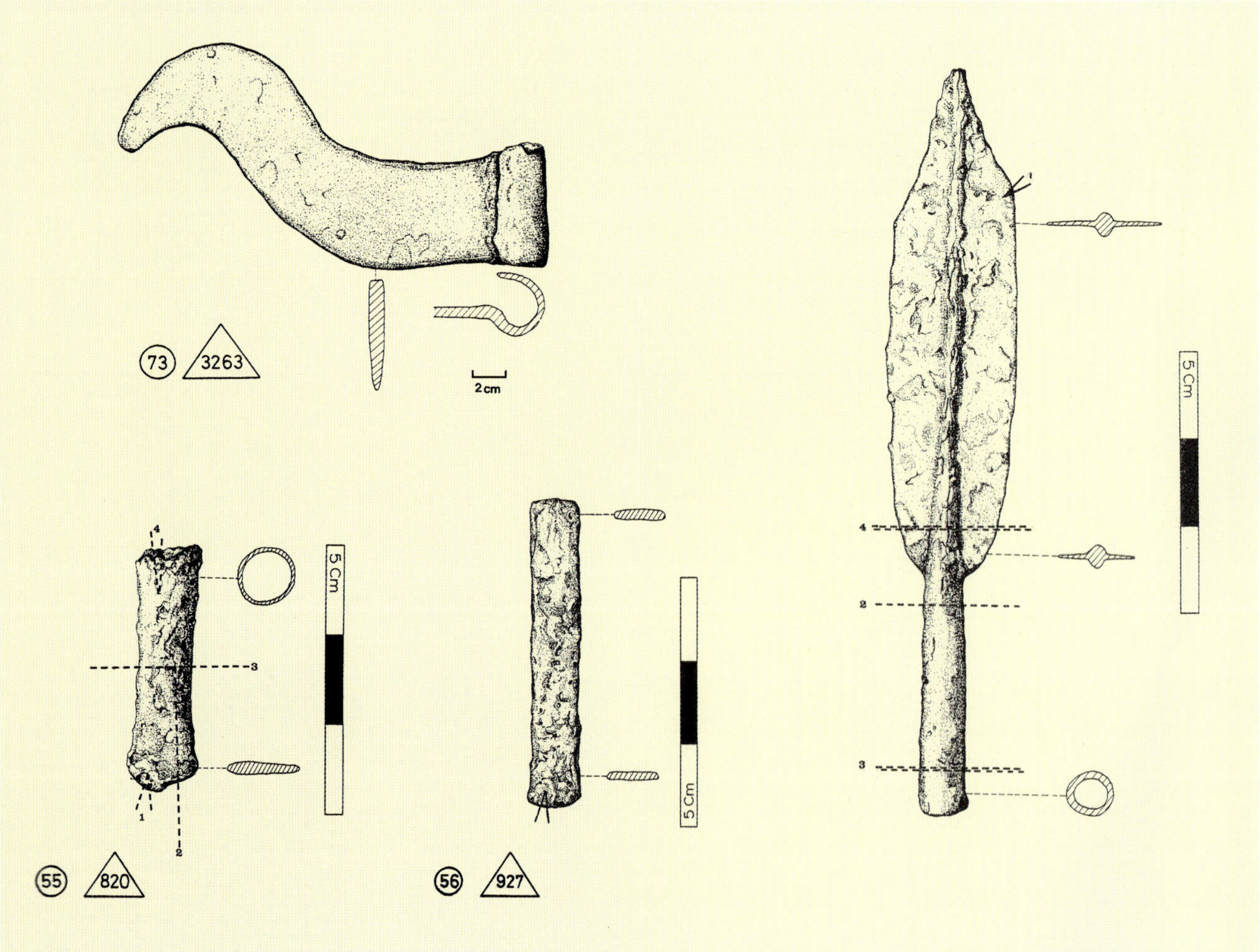

Fig. 1.74 Drawing of the iron tools from the iron age burial site of Ban Don Ta Phet.

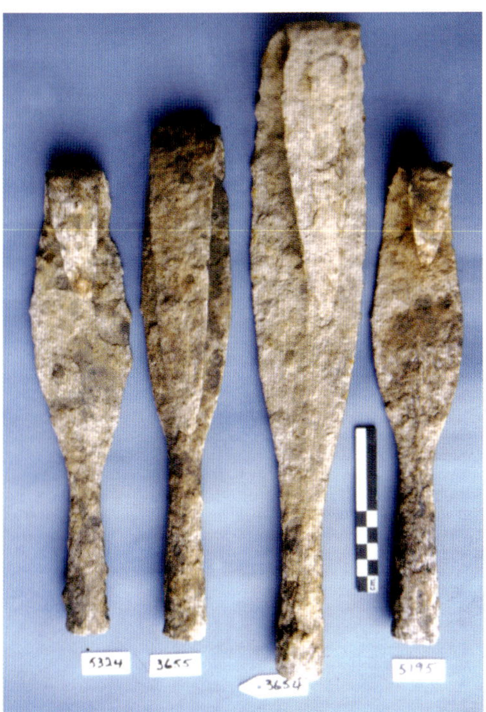

Figs. 1.75–1.76 Iron spears from Ban Don Ta Phet which were ritually killed by bending the blade prior to burial.

Fig. 1.77 Similar spearhead from the Samon Valley, Myanmar (Bennett 2013b).

Fig. 1.78a Iron billhook from mound at Ban Ta Po near Ban Kao National Museum.

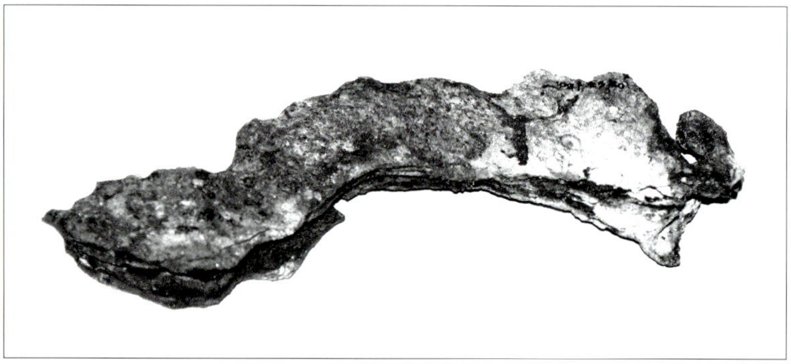

Fig. 1.78b Iron billhook from Khao Sam Kaeo. Courtesy Berenice Bellina.

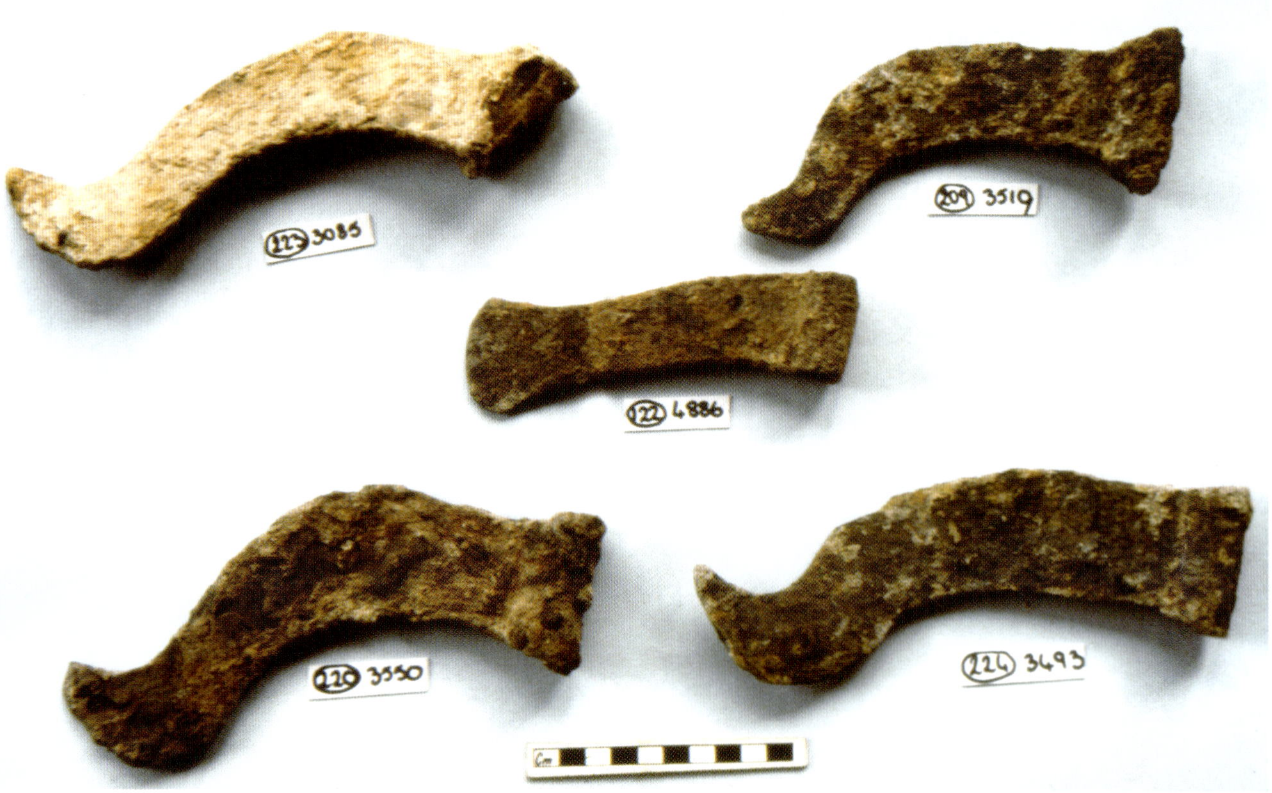

Fig. 1.79 Iron billhooks from Ban Don Ta Phet. BTP, KSK and BDTP have all produced characteristic high tin bronze bowls and hardstone beads (Figs. 1.41–1.45).

SEMIPRECIOUS STONE ORNAMENTS

Semiprecious Indian ornaments made of carnelian, agate and amethyst were certainly introduced from India where there had been a long tradition of bead making. They were subsequently produced by itinerant Indian craftsmen in Southeast Asia or perhaps were rapidly adapted by the indigenous craftsmen themselves. Bellina (2001, 2003, 2007; Bellina and Silapanth 2006) has demonstrated that the earliest stone beads were manufactured using Indian raw materials and Indian techniques and that these were then produced to suit the local taste providing a new category of prestige goods to satisfy the emerging elite. Within the district of U Thong, significant numbers of ancient beads have been found at forty-six settlement sites, twelve of which are within the ancient city walls (Pongpanich 2015).

Figs. 1.80–1.81 Semiprecious ornaments made of carnelian and agate were introduced from India. National Museum Bangkok, National Museum Ban Kao.

TRADE AND RELIGIOUS OBJECTS

It is likely that the quest for scarce and valuable raw materials like gold and tin, acted as major stimuli for the contact between India, Southeast Asia and China. These trade networks were used by Buddhist travellers and merchants who would have built shrines and temples in order to maintain their rituals of worship. By the first few centuries CE the first religious objects begin to appear in the archaeological record, and these Buddhist sacred symbols suggest that Indian religious influences were quite prevalent by this time. This would have brought a degree of cultural integration marking the infancy of the Indianized state and its religious ideology. Gold plaques recovered from consecrated deposits at Oc Eo, the port city of Funan, have more recently been excavated from several sites in southern Vietnam.[20] The site of Go Thap, dated from the early centuries CE to the eighth century, has produced some of the earliest known Brahmanical iconographic images in Southeast Asia, including three hundred and twenty-one gold plaques with simple incised decoration, depicting turtles representing Vishnu and his mount, the eagle Garuda, water buffaloes, elephants, snakes, conch shells, the sun, plants, and houses on stilts. The plaques were deposited as offerings together with five gold discs, three gold rings, a gold flower, eight precious stones and seven pieces of glass (Fig. 1.82–1.86) (Lê Thị Liên 2006, 2011, 2013). The site of Da Noi to the south west and dated to the fifth to eighth centuries CE has also produced similar plaques with incised decoration but with more complex designs and anthropomorphic images of Brahmanical deities (Figs. 1.87, 1.88).

The early centuries of the CE were not a process of Indian colonialisation. Rather, they witnessed a gradual and continuous cultural integration by which the political role of religion was sponsored by local rulers. The adoption of Dvaravati Buddhism, first by the elite and then disseminated to the wider society, created the ideal means of centralising power. Local rulers thus enhanced their status and furthered their sphere of influence.

According to Sri Lankan Buddhist tradition, monks were sent in small groups throughout South and Southeast Asia to propagate the Buddha's teaching during the reign of King Asoka (260–218 BCE) who had converted to Buddhism. One group was sent to '*Suvarnabhumi*: 'Land of Gold', which has been interpreted as Southeast Asia, especially Thailand and/or Lower Myanmar (the Irawaddy delta). Early forms of Buddhism practiced in Sri Lanka and Andhra Pradesh since at least the third century BCE, produced for example the Great Stupa at Amaravati. Buddhist symbols such as the triratna (Fig. 1.89) and the *bhaddapitha* or auspicious seat or throne (Fig. 1.66) are represented in gold jewellery recovered from early Pyu sites in Myanmar and from sites such as Khao Sam Keo and Bang Kluay Nok in southern Thailand. By the fourth to fifth centuries CE one of the most enduring symbols, that of the Wheel of the Law (*dharmacakra*) were mounted on stone pillars such as the one which was found near monument No.11 at U Thong (Brown 1996, 2014) (Figs. 1.90–1.92). These Wheels of the Law were manufactured at Dvaravati stone workshop sites such as the one excavated in Petchburi province (Indrawooth 2009)[21] but earlier examples of *dharmacakra* may well have been made of wood and no longer survive.

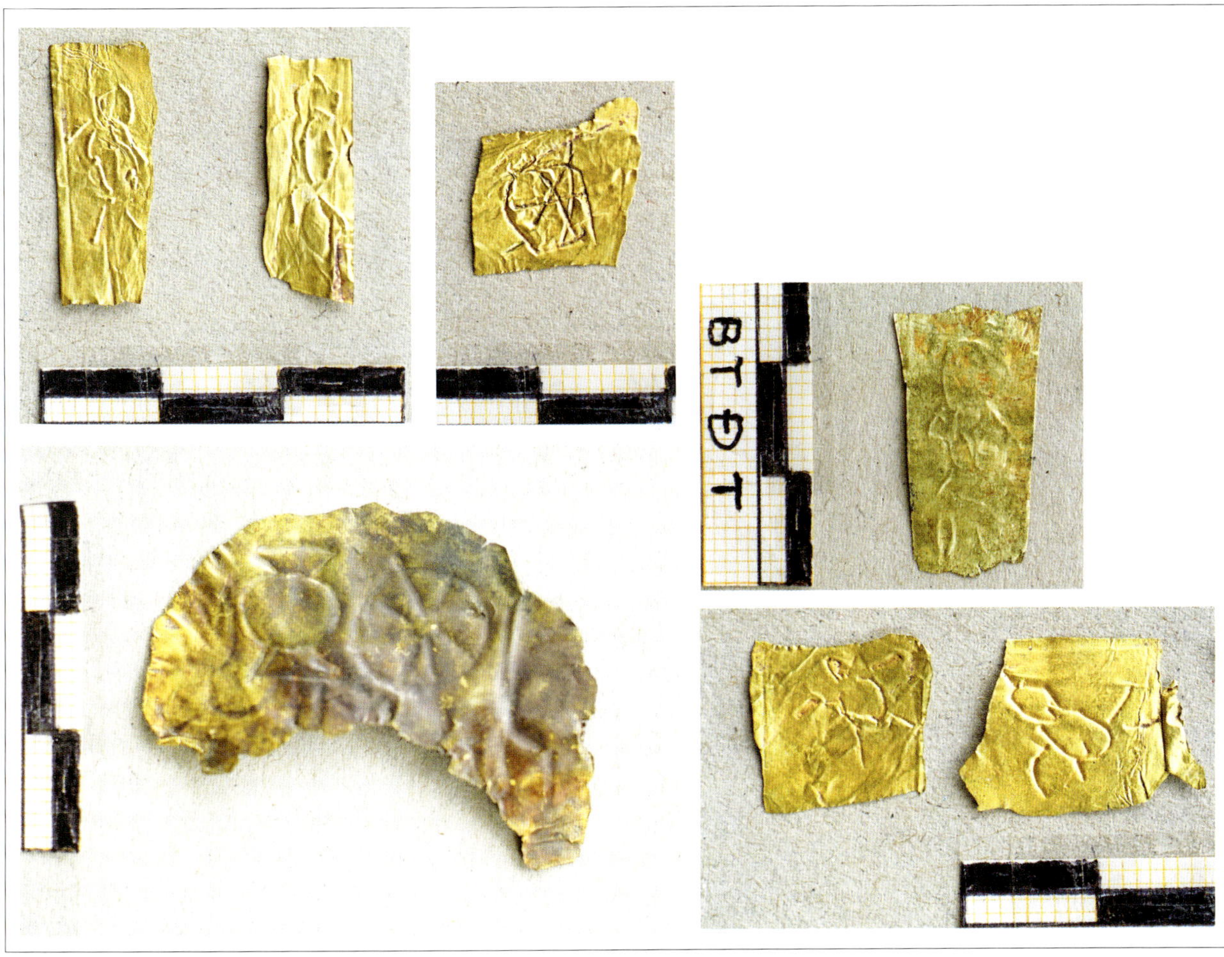

Figs. 1.82–1.86 Hammered gold plaques found *in situ* in a consecrated deposit at Go Thap in Dong Thap province. Courtesy Lê Thị Liên Lê Thị Liên.

Figs. 1.87–1.88 Hammered gold plaques with Brahmanical images and inscriptions of Sakhigcara and Vrahasghamni deposited as offerings at Da Noi in An Giang province. Excavated in 1985 from the architectural foundations. Courtesy Lê Thị Liên.

Fig. 1.89 Gold triratnas from Khao Sam Kaeo, SuthiRatana Foundation, Bangkok, KSK232, KSK355.

By the seventh to eighth centuries CE the extent of cultural intermixing is clear. Inscriptions in an adapted Indian post-Pallava alphabet as well as those in Sanskrit and Pali, together with coins in Pallava script are found in U Thong. A carved figure of Vishnu and a Linga from Khao Phra Mountain show that bramanical practices coexisted with Buddhism (Indrawooth 2004, Guy 2014). There is evidence of a monarchy in which Brahman priests performing Brahmanical rituals were sponsored by local rulers, their perogative being the consecration of kingship which provided a basis for the relationship between ruler and ruled.

By following the means by which Buddhism spread and co-opted local culture we can thread our way via commerce, travel and trade to the societal and political roles that were established. The Dvaravati period may be viewed as a political unit of indigenous people who adopted and integrated elements of Indian culture into their own distinctive way of life with Buddhism as an ideaology that was able to unify both culturally and politically the diverse communities which had co existed in the region for hundreds of years. U Thong embraced Buddhism, incorporating Brahmanical beliefs while the art, which responded continuously to the strong artistic tradition of local tastes, remained very distinctive from the Indian aesthetic (Indrawooth 2009).

Figs. 1.90–1.92 A *Dharmachakra*, the "wheel of the law" composed of a wheel, base and octagonal pole with a sitting deer which is thought to be the earliest representation of Buddhist teaching. This pillar was found near monument No.11 at U Thong and was probably manufactured at the Dvaravati stone workshop sites such as the ones excavated in Petchburi province (Indrawooth 2009).

1 Radiocarbon dates (uncalibrated) have also been published by Natapintu from excavations at U Thong, 2300 ± 310, 1790± 220, 1550±(reprinted in Lertrit 2001:231).

2 Some very well preserved stucco friezes from Khu Bua and Nakhon Pathon are on display at the National Museum Bangkok, the National Museum Rat Buri and the National Museum Nakhon Pathom.

3 A characteristic of Dvaravati moated sites is that they are often located near waterways which feed their moats and which typically have an irregular or oval plan (Gallon 2014).

4 The flood plains themselves would have been unsuitable for human settlement at this time.

5 The water networks linking U Thong to other communities included the river systems of the Mae Klong and the Tha Chin.

6 Three impressions from the same sixth century CE Indian terracotta property seal, one in U Thong museum (inv. no. 3/2520), the second also from U Thong and the third from Chansen, may have been the signature seal of a travelling Indian merchant.

7 A technique which can be further enhanced by the use of transplanting and water retention to allow double cropping.

8 The temper used in Dvaravati bricks was husked rice, indicating a high level of rice agriculture. This rice has been used in the carbon dating of some of the structures.

9 Brahmanism is the religious stream which developed from the ancient Vedas in India and which was spread through ritual by Brahmins. Its developed form after the eleventh century CE became known as Hinduism.

10 Other ancient polities included Muang Nong Jang, Muang Ku Muang, and Muang Suphan Buri (Pongpanich & Bhumadhon 2015:102).

11 At this time attempts were being made to establish a monarchy which would have incorporated both Brahmanical and Buddhist elements.

12 By the sixth century Funan had lost its power and influence, almost certainly due to a change in the navigation routes used within the South Seas and the corresponding decline of the ports in the Gulf of Thailand.

13 Other than in Vietnam and the eastern peninsula, *linglingo* ear ornaments have also been found in Cambodia, Sarawak, the Philippines, Taiwan, Japan and South Korea.

14 There are photos and a rubbing of another Roman coin found in Central Thailand (Glover oral communication).

15 The coin is that of an Emperor who ruled for only three years. The other coins of the Emperor Victorinus have all been found in the proximity of the mint in Cologne (Borell 2008a:14).

16 Ptolemy's information is derived from accounts written in the late first to early second century CE by the cartographer Marinus of Tyre which are now lost.

17 Hiranya is Sanskrit for gold

18 A recent survey by the National Institute of Statistics of mineral resources in Cambodia has identified 19 gold deposits (Bunker 2008: 301).

19 Archaeological excavations suggest that this was dry season metal working.

20 Fourth to sixth century CE inscriptions on gold plaques have been found at: Go Thap in Dong Thap province where gold plaques were found in situ in a consecrated deposit; Da Noi in An Giang province, where gold plaques with Brahmanical images and inscriptions were excavated in 1985 from architectural foundations; Go Xoai in Long An province, a satellite site of Oc Eo, where an inscribed Buddhist mantra in the shape of a page of a palm leaf manuscript and gold plaques were excavated in 2001 (Skilling 1999). At Cat Tien in Lam Dong province, dated to late seventh to the end of the eighth century CE, excavations between 1994 and 1997 and 2001 and 2003 unearthed gold plaques with depictions of Indian gods and goddesses and texts in a central sanctum under the main foundation (Lê Thị Liên and Witzel and 2013; Lê Thị Liên 2014).

21 A total of three Dharmachakras have been found in U Thong.

CHAPTER 2

ANCIENT GOLD MATERIALS AND MANUFACTURING TECHNIQUES

INTRODUCTION

Fig. 2.2 Buddha head and foot found at U Thong Monument 2. The head was deposited in the northwest corner of the terrace while the foot was found beneath the western entrance.

Opposite page
Fig. 2.1 Director of U Thong National Museum pointing to the find spot of the Dvaravati hinged ear ornament which found in the grounds of the museum during construction work in 2010.

The ancient gold that we know today may have been placed in rich burials to honour the dead,[1] deliberately concealed in hoards for safe keeping in times of danger and never subsequently recovered, or have been accidentally lost or misplaced. The hinged split ear ornament (cat. no. 5) was a lone find recovered in 2010 during construction work in the U Thong museum compound within the ancient city, and was presumably accidentally lost by its wearer (Fig. 2.1). Other items may have been deposited under temple floors as an offering or consecration or placed in the upper levels of the towers of a religious sanctuary. The Buddha head and foot (Fig. 2.2) (cat. nos. 1 and 2) were recovered during the restoration of Monument 2 at U Thong in 1963 by the Supan Buri Fine Arts Department. Although both the head and the foot were found within the same monument, the head had been deposited on the terrace near the northwest corner, while the foot was found beneath the western entrance (Fine Arts Department 2002). At Wat Phu, Champassak in Laos, gold dust and small grains were found as offerings; at Phimai in Nakhon Ratchasima in Northeast Thailand a gold diadem, pectoral and ear ornaments were recovered under a laterite slab and are now displayed in Phimai Museum; and at Go Thap and Da Noi in southern Vietnam hundreds of hammered gold plaques with incised decoration had been deposited as offerings (*Lê Thị Liên* 2008) (Figs. 1.82–1.86). The Dvaravati gold objects which are displayed in the U Thong and Bangkok National Museums and the objects in private collections, have almost without exception been discovered accidentally (Fig. 2.3), either during construction work accompanying the

Fig. 2.3 The majority of gold is found as chance finds and will be melted down.

urbanisation of the rural landscape, by farmers ploughing or by people working in the fields. In some cases objects may be sold on the international art market. An example is the Auytthaya period gold crown (Fig. 2.4), which is now in a private American collection but was reportedly found near U Thong in the 1980's. In many cases the gold will simply be melted down for its metal value and estimates suggest that perhaps less than 5% of the gold that once circulated in Southeast Asia survives (Reinecke 2015).[2]

Fig. 2.4 An Auytthaya period gold crown, private collection USA.

Some practising archaeologists prefer on principle to ignore all objects that do not derive from officially documented excavations. But in the case of Southeast Asian gold this approach is simply not practicable, since the vast majority of objects both in museums (Figs. 2.5, 2.6, 2.8 & 2.9) and private collections (Fig. 2.7) are the result of chance findings and most lack any provenance whatsoever.[3]

Fig. 2.5 Gold figure of *Kiratimukha,* National Museum U Thong, 10/274/2509.

Fig. 2.6 Gold figure of *Kinnari,* National Museum U Thong, 10/275/2509.

Fig 2.7 Dvaravati gold from U Thong in Khun Suriya Surapanich's private collection.

Fig. 2.8 Dvaravati gold pendant. Chance find donated to UThong National Museum in 1950.

Fig 2.9 Dvaravati gold pendant from U Thong displayed at Bangkok National Museum.

Fig. 2.10 Villagers today dredging for gold on the Tenasserim River near Dawei in Myanmar.

Most metallic gold in today's world is retrieved by the deep mining of primary hard rock deposits but in the prehistoric and early historic periods gold would undoubtedly have been extracted by panning alluvial sediments. The technique requires little capital investment in equipment and no specialist technology. Villagers today can still be seen panning and dredging for gold using the same simple methods (Figs. 2.10, 2.11) and the economic viability of the panning or dredging will be determined by the price of gold on the international market. When gold prices are at their highest it becomes more economically advantageous to pan the gold bearing streams and the villagers sell their gold to middlemen who themselves sell it to merchants (Figs. 2.12–2.14). The author has also observed goldsmiths in Myanmar using locally panned gold to produce replica ancient beads (Figs. 2.15–2.17).

Figs. 2.11–2.14 Villagers on the Tenasserim River near Dawei in Myanmar selling their gold to middlemen.

Figs. 2.15–2.17 Goldsmith in Myanmar using locally panned gold to produce replica ancient beads. He blows air through a blow pipe thus increasing the rate of flow of oxygen which intensifies the heat of the oil lamp flame.

Gold panned from the rivers of Sarawak in Borneo has been found to contain traces of antimony with platinum and arsenic suggesting that in the twelth century western Borneo was producing gold and transporting it to the Malay peninsula (Treloar 1977). Gold from Sulawesi is characterized by the presence of nickel as the only impurity (Fabris and Treloar 1980, Stambolov 1999) and gold from Sumatra has been found to contain tin, lead, and mercury. Provenance studies on the gold finds from Kota Cina in Northeastern Sumatra have attempted to locate the source of gold by examining the composition of finished gold sheet (Manning, McKinnon and Trelor 1980; Swan and Scott 1990). However, sources of gold would have included recycled, damaged or obsolete objects which may themselves have contained other metals such as copper. Impurity patterns are far from clear and this creates almost insurmountable difficulties is attempting to provenance ancient gold. Studies of early material will have a greater chance of success since it is less likely to have been reused—the possibility of matching an object to its source decreases exponentially with the degree of processing and recycling that the object has undergone.

Wherever it is found alluvial and mined gold from primary vein deposits will invariably contain 5 to 40% silver and 0.1 to 1.5% copper by weight as the major impurities. There is evidence that early Asian explorers were aware of the differences in gold compositions, and an eleventh-century Indian text refers to gold from *Survarnadvipa* as being of different types: yellow gold colour and white shell colour, which presumably refers to the amounts of silver or copper contained in the alloy. An eleventh-century Sanskrit inscription of a Cham king by the name Rudravarman III found at Po-Nagar temple in Kauthara, near modern Nha Trang in Vietnam, mentions a donation by the king of seven *panas* of red coloured gold (*rakta kaladhautam*) and 23 *kattikas* and two *panas* of superior white gold (*sitatara kaladhautam*).[4] Gold can be used as found, purified to remove the naturally occurring silver and copper, or debased by the addition of silver and copper for fraudulent purposes or in times of economic difficulty. Some goldsmiths would have had particular technical requirements of their metal, causing them to seek gold of a particular purity. Gold that is very pure is also very soft and would have been chosen for the manufacture of the thin hammered gold such as that often used for foundation deposits or for hammered gold beads. Other objects were alloyed with a greater percentage of silver and copper in order to harden them, thus producing the desired mechanical and physical properties required for their purpose.[5]

For Southeast Asia there is as yet little analytical data concerning the chemical characterization of the gold alloys used. However, recent excavations at the protohistoric cemetery of Prohear, about 65 km east of Phnom Penh and 40 km west of the Vietnamese border, dated to between the second century BCE and the first century CE, have provided the first significant corpus of provenanced scientifically excavated early gold material for analysis (Reinecke & Vin Laychour, Seng Soneta 2009; Reinecke 2012, 2015). Fifty-nine out of the seventy-nine gold objects excavated from fifty two burials have been analysed using LA-ICP-MS (laser ablation inductively coupled plasma mass spectrometry) to obbtain detailed information about their composition and trace element pattern (Schlosser, Reinecke, Schwab, Pernicka, Sonetra & Vin Laychour 2012). The data indicates that slightly less than half the objects, which were mostly small wire spiral rings, contained more silver than gold, suggesting that the inhabitants of Prohear were using a native panned electrum as well as making intentional alloys. The natural electrums contained 35 to 44% silver and less than 0.2% copper, while the intentional alloys contained the same low copper content but a higher silver content of 56 to 68%.[6] Further, the data based on differences in the Platinum, Iridium and Bismuth levels and Palladium to Platinum ratios suggested that objects which appeared non local in design and which were associated with the richer more elite burials had a different trace element fingerprint to those items thought to be of local origin.

Riederer (1994: 49) analyzed objects from the Thompson Collection of Javanese gold, now in the Yale University Art Gallery (Miksic 1990, 2011), and although this material is not from a secure provenance and the analyses varied considerably, he has suggested that the earlier items in the collection contained a higher ratio of silver to gold.

Because gold, silver and copper all melt together to form a complete solid solution series, an entire range of alloy compositions is technically possible. However, once gold was being used as a measure of wealth, it would have become essential to not only standardize the weights but, at least to some extent to control the composition of gold by adding or removing other metals. The earliest reference to the removal of silver from gold, known as cementation, is contained in an ancient Indian text known as the *Kautiliya,* which is believed to have been written by the scholar *Arthasastra* for the chief minister of the Mauryean Emperor Chandragupta, who ruled northern India in the fourth century BCE (Kangle 1960). Gold dust or thin hammered sheets were placed in acidic salts, which attacked the silver and formed a silver chloride vapour, leaving a purified gold metal. To quote the *Kautilya Arthasastra*:

> *"Ornamental gold of the best kind, possessed of excellent color, passed through an equal amount of lead, turned into leaves by heating made bright with Indus-earth, becomes the base of blue, yellow, white, green and parrot-feather colors[7]".*

It is unclear to what extent goldsmiths undertook the process of removing base metal oxides by the addition of lead to a crucible of molten gold, known as cupellation. This relatively straightforward process involves oxidising lead using a blast of cold air so that the base metal oxides are absorbed into the lead oxide, leaving only the silver remaining in the gold. Touchstones were certainly part of the goldsmiths' tool set and examples have been found at Kota Cina in Northeastern Sumatra (Swan and Scott 1990) and at Khuan Lukpat, a third to sixth CE site on the west coast of southern Thailand in Krabi Province, also called Klong Tom (Fig. 2.18). This touchstone dates to the third century CE and has a Tamil inscription (*Perumpadan Kal*) identifying it as the property of Perumpadan (Srisuchat 1996: 250). This is one of the earliest Brahmi inscriptions found in Thailand indicating that Indian goldsmiths were operating in this region at an early date.

Fig. 2.18 Goldsmith's touchstone, third century CE, Khlong Thom Phra Kru Athan Sankarakit Museum, Krabi.

The site of Khuan Lukpat has also produced hundreds of gold coins, twelve of which have been examined (Figs. 2.19–2.21). The occurrence of so many gold coins together with the touchstone, several Roman tin coin imitation pendants and their corresponding stone moulds and many waste gold fragments indicate that this was an early production site (Bronson 1990:213). Seven of the gold coins are struck with a conch shell motif oone side; two have a *Srivatsa* on the other side while the others are blank; two have an as yet unidentified roman emperor on the obverse and an unidentified script on the reverse,[8] one coin is completely blank on both sides; and one half coin has a *Srivatsa* on one side and is blank on the other. There are two different sizes of coin: the larger weighs approximately 0.9 g, while the smaller weighs between 0.4 g and 0.6 g (Fig. 2.21). The Pyu of Myanmar are thought to have had a gold coinage in addition to the huge numbers of 5th–9 th century CE silver Rising Sun and Conch coins, although none have so far been found.[9] A Chinese text known as the *Xin Tang Shu* (New Tang History) compiled by Ouyang Xia and others, written in the eleventh century CE refers to a Pyu gold coinage and although Wicks (1992) has suggested that this is a copyist's addition,[10] the recent finds from Khuan Lukpad may refute this.

In general, the composition of the gold jewellery and artefacts in societies that did not use a gold monetary system or in which the gold was not centrally controlled, has been found to be much more random, varying from 45 to 99 percent gold, than in cultures where coins were widely circulated or where gold was used for fines or in settling disputes. By the time of the Khmer king Jayavarman V in the ninth century CE, punishments were according to the rank of the offender and royal princes were being fined twenty pala of gold (Majumdar 1953:268–9).

Figs. 2.19–2.20 Gold coins from Khuan Lukpat, west peninsula Thailand, SuthiRatana Foundation, Bangkok.

11.13 x 10.18 mm
MT: 1.10 mm
Wt: 0.94 g

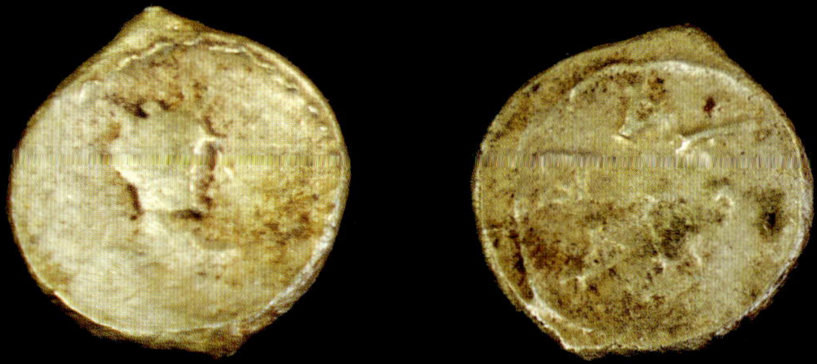

KLP 089.1

7.40 x 8.03 mm
MT: 1.08 mm
Wt: 0.48 g

KLP 089.2

7.34 x 8.04 mm
MT: 1.37 mm
Wt: 0.53 g

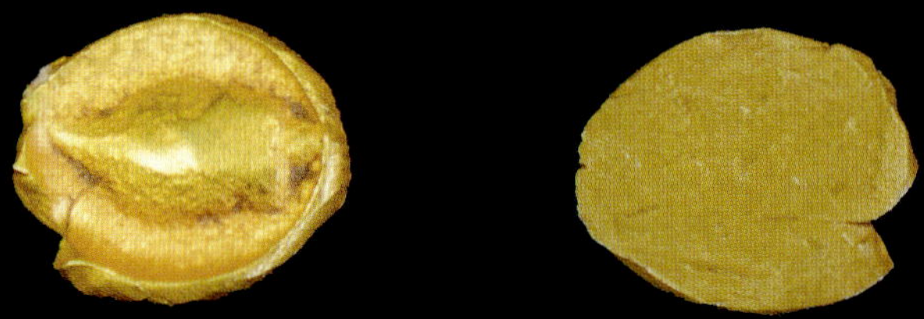

KLP 089.3

7.86 x 7.32 mm
MT: 1.16 mm
Wt: 0.44 g

KLP 089.4

Fig. 2.21 Gold coins from Khuan Lukpat, SuthiRatana Foundation, Bangkok.

7.57 x 7.72 mm
MT: 1.04 mm
Wt: 0.46 g

KLP137.1

9.44 x 7.49 mm
MT: 1.42 mm
Wt: 0.91 g

KLP137.2

5.28 x 9.87 mm
MT: 1.18 mm
Wt: 0.42 g

KLP512

11.44 x 9.64 mm
MT: 0.62 mm
Wt: 0.99 g

KLP436.1

Fig 2.21 Gold coins from Khuan Lukpat, SuthiRatana Foundation, Bangkok.

8.27 x 8.31 mm
MT: 1.19 mm
Wt: 0.49 g
KLP436.2

7.85 x 9.13 mm
MT: 0.99 mm
Wt: 0.39 g
KLP166.1

7.01 x 4.31 mm
MT: 0.38 mm
Wt: 0.06 g
KLP166.2

4.85 x 12.50 mm
MT: 0.71 mm
Wt: 0.38 g
KLP132

Fig 2.21 Gold coins from Khuan Lukpat, SuthiRatana Foundation, Bangkok

MANUFACTURING TECHNIQUES

Goldsmiths themselves would rarely if ever have been able to acquire sufficient capital to control their own stocks of metal and they would typically have obtained their gold, probably in the form of scrap (Figs. 1.63, 2.22) from the wealthy individual, the temple or the institution that had commissioned the desired article. Inscriptions at Indravarmen's ninth-century temple of Prea Ko describe offerings of gold and silver and there are references to ironsmiths, moulders of statues, sewers of leaves, basket makers, perfume grinders, spinners, and weavers, but there is no specific mention of a guild of goldsmiths. An inscription dated to 927, from the reign of Jayavarman V, refers to a corporation of goldsmiths (Majumdar 1953: 319), but there is no indication of whether the temples employed them.[11] Neither the Chinese envoy Zhou Daguan who visited the Khmer complex of Angkor during 1295–96 CE or the Khmer temple inscriptions or the jewellery itself tell us about the identity of these craftsmen.

If the inscriptions cannot reveal information concerning the identity, status, organisation and production system of goldsmiths, then it is to the objects themselves that we must pose such questions as, how did the jeweller procure his gold? For whom was he making the items? What was the extent of state and/or religious control? Was there an uncontrolled private system? What was the goldsmith's social status? Was there a guild structure? Did the goldsmith work in isolation or in a workshop? Were these workshops in residential areas, religious compounds, or both? Were there masters and apprentices? What were the range of techniques employed and did they differ sufficiently to allow differentiation between workshops?

Fig. 2.22 Scrap gold recovered from Khao Sam Kaeo, east peninsula Thailand. SuthiRatana Foundation, Bangkok.

HAMMERING

The simple mechanical hammering out of gold is the most logical first step in the production of an object. The first step would have entailed the casting of a piece of gold, which would then have been repeatedly hammered and annealed until the required reduction in thickness was achieved. Due to this repeated hammering it is often possible to see the separation of the gold layers in sheet gold (Fig. 2.23).

Fig. 2.23 Separation of the gold layers within a hammered sheet.

The earliest documented excavated gold objects in Southeast Asia are beads made from gold sheet, found in funerary contexts at the coastal Sa Huynh sites of Go Ma Voi and Go Mun in southern Vietnam, dated to the third to second centuries BCE. These beads were clearly highly prized and were found associated with exotic goods including agate, nephrite and quartz beads, *linglingo* earrings, and a bimetallic axe (Reinecke & Nguyen Thi Thanh Luyen 2009). These sites are on the banks of Ba Ren river, a branch of the Thu Bon, near Hoi An in central Vietnam, and are linked by river to Kham Duc, 65 km northeast, an area where gold is still mined today and where ancient shafts have been reported (Reinecke oral communication).

Gold sheet may be simply left as a thin hammered edge or the excess gold simply be folded over onto the reverse (Fig. 2.24). The Buddha head and foot (Fig. 2.2) (cat. nos. 1 & 2) were constructed from several pieces of hammered gold sheet and the edges were simply finished by hammering the excess metal onto the reverse. In cases where the gold required cutting this was invariably achieved with a straight-edged chisel.

Fig. 2.24 Excess gold folded over on to the reverse of the gold sheet.

The date at which scissors were introduced to Southeast Asia is unclear but it is generally accepted that they were not used in protohistoric or early historic times.[11] An engraved line is sometimes visible immediately adjacent to a cut edge indicating that shapes were pre-planned and were first drawn out using an engraving tool prior to the cutting of the metal. The marking out prior to cutting can be clearly seen on the thick hammered gold sheet from Khao Sam Kaeo (KSK 258) (Fig.2.25–2.27).

Gold was shaped by pressing it down into negative moulds or onto positive moulds known as formers, made of wood, stone or metal. It could be hammered directly onto a soft support material such as pitch, resin or even lead metal which would allow the goldsmith to work freehand without the constraints of a predetermined mould. The pressing into or onto a mould would have been achieved using simple hammers and punches or, in the case of thin gold, it could be pressed down using blocks of resin or lead. Hollow sheet gold objects would have been too frail if left hollow and were filled with clay or resin to add strength. In the case of the Buddha head (Fig. 2.2) (cat. 1), the gold sheet was probably hammered directly over the clay model which would have provided the required support during and after manufacture. The Dvaravati gold pendant (Figs. 2.28 & 2.29) (cat. 3) was probably made by hammering the metal into a negative die such as the stone mould on display in the National Museum of U Thong (Fig. 2.30). This mould is clearly not for casting liquid metal since unlike the other moulds shown in Fig. 2.31 and those in 2.35, 2.36 and 2.38 there is no provision for a pouring channel.

Weight: 0.75 g
Width: 20.31 mm
Height: 22.24 mm
Elemental composition: 85.66% gold, 13.86% silver, 0.07% copper, 0.40% tin

Figs. 2.25–2.27 Thick hammered gold sheet with an open-work design cut out using a chisel. The areas to be cut were marked out prior to cutting. 5th–3rd BCE, Khao Sam Kaeo, east peninsula Thailand, SuthiRatana Foundation, Bangkok, KSK 258.

Figs. 2.28, 2.29 Gold pendant made by hammering gold into a negative die, National Museum U Thong, 10/88/2503.

Figs. 2.30–2.31 Stone moulds for the manufacture of decorated hammered sheet in the collection of the National Museum U Thong.

Figs. 2.32 Reverse of the gold fragments with animal decorative motif, Khao Sam Kaeo, east peninsula Thailand, SuthiRatana Foundation, Bangkok, KSK 512.

Gold foil fragments with an animal decorative motif (Figs. 2.32–2.35) and interlinked 'S' motif[12] were recovered in 2015 from a sand quarry on the Tha Tapao River at Khao Sam Kaeo. To achieve these intricate designs the gold would have been worked over a decorated mould, possibly of wood or bone but more likely of stone, since a harder material would have facilitated the precision and detailed achieved. The gold is extremely thin (0.38 mm in thickness) and the object would have required a backing material, although no evidence or trace of such a material remains (Fig. 2.32).

These gold fragments were found associated with a ringstone also with an animal decorative motif although not an identical one (Figs. 2.36–2.39). These finds perhaps suggest that ringstones may have, among other things been used as moulds for gold working and the beating of thin gold sheet ornaments. The ringstone itself is carved in a stone which is soft enough to allow ease of carving but hard enough and with a small grain size to have facilitated the precision of detailed decoration.

Ringstones are characteristic of the Mauryan-Sunga periods of Northern India and the example from KSK is the only one known as yet to have been found outside the Indian subcontinent.

Weight: 0.57 g
MT: 0.38 mm
Composition: 84.49% gold, 12.06% silver, 2.6% copper (traces of iron, titanium and silica which were picked up from the soil still attached to areas of the gold).
Find location: Khao Sam Kaeo hill KSK 258.

Fig. 2.33–2.35 Front and details of the gold fragments with an animal decorative motif, 2nd BCE or earlier. Khao Sam Kaeo, east peninsula Thailand, SuthiRatana Foundation, Bangkok, KSK 512.

Figs. 2.36–2.39 Ringstone carved in a hard fine grained stone, Diameter: 5.8 cm, Khao Sam Kaeo. Intricately carved on the upper face with two bands of cable-moulding between which a ring of animals and birds: lion, goose; stag, antelope, goose; deer, horse, taurine, stag, antelope, goose and ram run towards the right separated by four floral designs. Within the central hole are four standing nude female figures often interpreted without any certainty as a "fertility goddess", alternating with a foliated design, representing the Indian 'Honey suckle' or 'Tree of Life and Fortune' *(Kalpavriksha or Kalpadruma)*. The reverse face is blank but bears what appears to be a scratched inscription. SuthiRatana Foundation, Bangkok, KSK522.

CASTING

The other method of manufacture, that of casting, was achieved either by the lost wax technique or by pouring gold into finely carved open or two-piece stone moulds, made of a close-grained sandstone which would ensure the reproduction of the carved detail in the metal (Fig. 2.40–2.42). The two halves of the moulds were linked using pins placed in drilled holes near the edge of the mould and hot metal poured in through channels, known as casting sprues. For the case of complex three-dimensional objects with undercutting in the form, wax models were made. The models were coated in clay investment and then heated, so that the wax melted out of the investment and liquid metal could be poured in to take its place, thus reproducing the exact details of the wax model. In cases where multiple copies were required, individual components of the wax models would themselves have been cast in stone moulds.

Casting was one of the main methods for manufacturing Southeast Asian jewellery and was used far more frequently than it was in the classical world, where gold ornaments were much more likely to have been made by the more time consuming but less wasteful and less costly technique of hammering. Casting required the goldsmith to have access to a surplus of gold metal, since an allowance would have to have been made for the excess metal required in the casting sprues.

Fig. 2.41 Sandstone mould from Khao Sam Kaeo, east peninsula Thailand, SuthiRatana Foundation, Bangkok.

That casting was the preferred method of manufacture is probably due to the means by which the goldsmiths obtained their gold. It is unlikely that the artisans themselves would have had the capital to hold stocks of gold, and objects would have been commissioned on an individual basis with patrons supplying their own gold in the form of scrap or ingots. If, as we suspect, gold in the Khmer Empire was centrally controlled, the required excess metal would have been of little consequence, since it would simply have been melted down and reused in subsequent castings and this may explain why so much of the Khmer gold is cast.

Fig. 2.42 Sandtone mould for casting from Khao Sam Kaeo, east peninsula Thailand, Chumphon National Museum.

Inscribed Javanese finger rings were cast as blanks which were then chased or engraved and polished (Fig. 2.54). Among the blank undecorated examples of rings that have been recovered, some still have the rough-casting skin, suggesting that local work shops applied the decoration on demand. In other examples the decoration itself appears to have been cast-in with no subsequent reworking of the design.

It is not always straightforward or even possible to distinguish between methods of manufacture, as is the case for the coin pendant shown in figs. 1.59–1.62 in Chapter 1.

Fig. 2.43 Stone mould for a portrait pendant. The mould has no pouring channel. Phu Khao Thong, west peninsula Thailand, SuthiRatana Foundation, Bangkok.

Top of the page
Fig. 2.40 Sandtone moulds for casting, National Museum U Thong.

JOINING

Gold jewellery items were often made by assembling separate components which, depending on the effects required and the complexities of the design, were themselves an assortment of cast and hammered elements. The individual components of hammered objects were often assembled by mechanical means rather than through the use of solder. The Buddha head and foot (cat. no. 1 & 2) were largely assembled by mechanical means (Figs. 2.44, 2.45), although the ears were soldered onto the head (Fig. 2.46). Attachments on the reverse of jewellery were usually made separately and soldered on (Fig. 2.47), while the use of a carbon compound mixed with organic glue appears to have been entirely confined to the decorative technique of granulation (see p. 70–71).

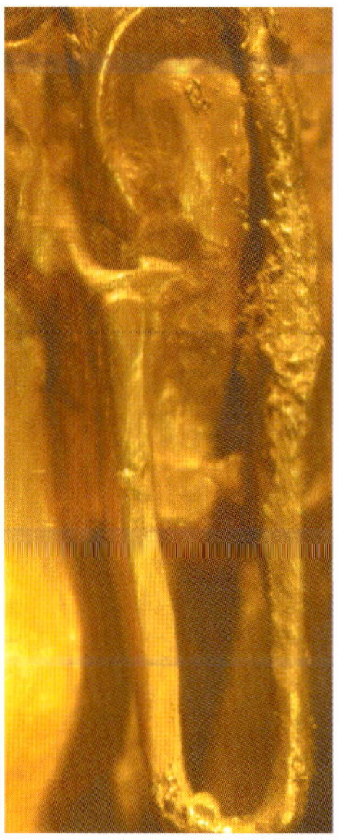

Fig. 2.46 The ears of the Buddha (cat. no 1) were attached using solder.

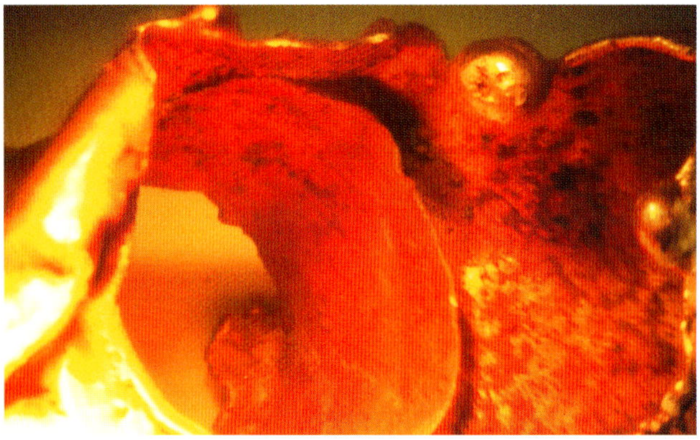

Figs. 2.44, 2.45 The Buddha foot and ankle were simply mechanically joined by fitting a sleeve of gold into the ankle opening.

Fig. 2.47 The attachment on the *kiratimukha* (cat. no. 9) was made separately and soldered onto the reverse.

WIRE

The use of thin strands of metal wire is a universal design feature in gold working. A piece of gold can be worked into a long thin strand either by hammering, twisting and rolling, or pulling the wire through a series of holes of decreasing diameter in an iron or steel draw plate. Drawn wire has an even circular section and is characterised by parallel striations that follow the axis of the wire. It is used predominantly in jewellery of the later periods and fragments have been excavated at the twelfth-century workshop site of Kota Cina in Northeastern Sumatra (Swan and Scott 1990). Later Classic period Javanese jewellery may well have been influenced by the increasing trade with the Islamic world after about 1000 CE although Ogden (2004) has identified drawn wire in early Korean gold working of the Silla Kingdom (fifth to sixth centuries), which may suggest that wire drawing was introduced from the Far East rather than the Islamic world. Wire drawing certainly seems possible by the end of the T'ang Period in China and was widespread by the thirteenth to fourteenth centuries CE. Since wire drawing was certainly not widespread until towards the end of the first millennium CE, all ancient gold wire will show evidence of casting or hammering and folding, as seen on the earring, bead, garment toggle and ring (Figs. 2.48–2.52, 2.61). Indeed the type of wire and the appearance of the ends of the wire can often provide valuble clues as to the authenticity of ancient jewellery.

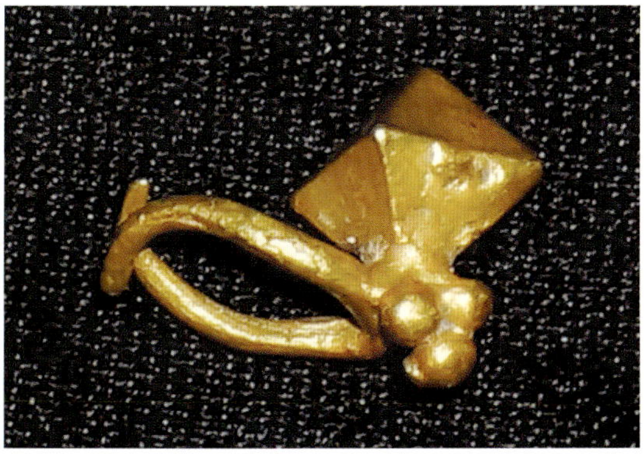

Fig 2.48 Hammered wire used for earring attachment, cat. no. 21, private collection U Thong.

Fig 2.50 Cast wire used in garment toggle construction, cat. no. 18, private collection U Thong.

Fig 2.49 Hammered wire used for bead, cat. no. 31. National Museum Bangkok.

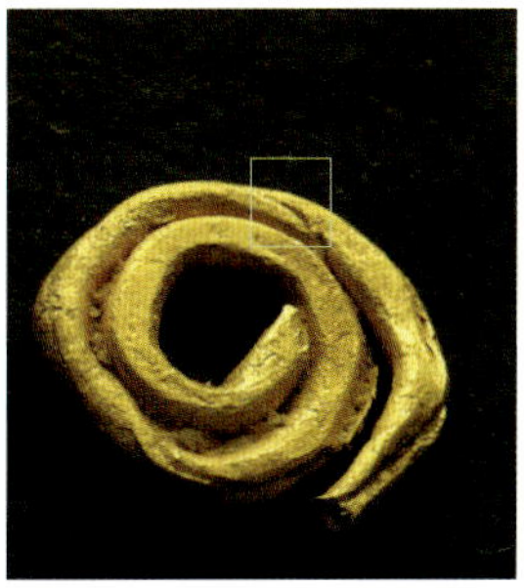

Figs. 2.51, 2.52 Wire wrapped ring, KSK 381 and coil of hammered wire, KSK 282. The spiral from folding and twisting the gold sheet to form the wire is clearly visible. Khao Sam Kaeo, SuthiRatana Foundation, Bangkok.

DECORATION: PUNCHING, ENGRAVING, GRANULATION

Decoration of gold surfaces will often involve the use of small chisels, which are tapped into the gold surface with a hammer to produce single punches or connected lines. The hair on the Buddha's head (cat. 1) has been achieved by depressing the gold into the soft clay core, using a simple punch to achieve the required design (Fig. 2.53). A straight chisel-like chaser will sometimes be used to produce curved lines; this results in a characteristic feathering pattern with jagged edges in the curved areas, caused by manipulating a straight-edged tool around corners (Fig. 2.54). Chasing, rather than engraving, was often used for decorating thin gold sheet such as the designs of Sakhigiara and Vrahasghanni on the gold plaques found at Da Noi in southern Vietnam (Figs. 1.87–1.88). Chasing differs from engraving which involves using a sharper tool which cuts out and removes metal, leaving characteristic parallel lines within the grooves, rather than depressing and deforming it. Because of this engraving is not suitable for use on thin gold sheet but will be the most effective method for producing deep inscriptions on cast gold such as the gold seal from Bang Kluay Nok (Figs. 1.65–1.68).

A decorative technique used abundantly in Southeast Asian jewellery entails the application of small gold spheres in rows or in fields (Fig. 2.55).[13] The earliest documented granulation in Southeast Asia was found at the late centuries BCE Sa Huynh site of Giong Ca Vo in southern Vietnam and Reinecke (2015) has also described an earring from Prohear with granulation. Numerous beads with granulation, similar to those in the National Museum Bangkok (Figs. 2.57–2.58), have been found at Khao Sam Kaeo (Fig. 2.56) (Pryce, Bellina and Bennett 1986) and Phu Khao Thong, both production centres and trading ports on the western peninsula of southern Thailand, and at the sites of Klong Nou and Aou Yai near Victoria Point in southern Myanmar.

Fig. 2.53 Hair on the Buddha head, cat.no. 1 was achieved by simple chasing.

Fig. 2.54 A straight chasing tool used in curved areas results in a characteristic feathering pattern.

Fig. 2.55 Pendant with granulation, cat no.32. National Museum Bangkok.

Fig. 2.56 Central knobbed and polyhedral gold beads from Khao Sam Kaeo, SuthiRatana Foundation, Bangkok.

A particularly fine example of granulation is shown on the lion head bead from the early CE site of Ban Bang Kluay Nok on the peninsula which is completely covered in tiny gold orbs of varying size (Figs. 2.59–2.61).

Granules are produced by melting small pieces of gold which, by force of surface tension, will invariably form round solid balls, since this is the form with the smallest surface area. During the process the balls must be kept seperate, since if they join they will coalesce to form one larger ball. Once cooled the spheres are sorted into sizes and are then stuck onto gold sheet using a mixture of a powdered copper compound and an organic adhesive. When the assemblage is heated, the glue burns to carbon and the copper compound is reduced in situ to copper metal, which diffuses into the surrounding gold. A copper/gold alloy bond is formed directly at the point of contact between the granules and the gold sheet, thus forming an almost invisible join (Fig. 2.58). Because thick cast gold will conduct heat so rapidly that the gold granules would be liable to melt before they were fused into place, granulation is almost invariably confined to the decorating of thin sheet. Modern copies of objects with granulation will often have tell-tale signs of the use of solder which is fused with the aid of a borax flux. The solder surrounds the granules so that they are embedded and the solder can be seen up the sides of the granules which will not have the completely round shape of true granulation.

Fig. 2.57 Polyhedral beads with granulation, cat.no. 31. National Museum Bangkok.

Fig. 2.58 Photomicrograph showing the join between the gold granules and the main structure of the bead.

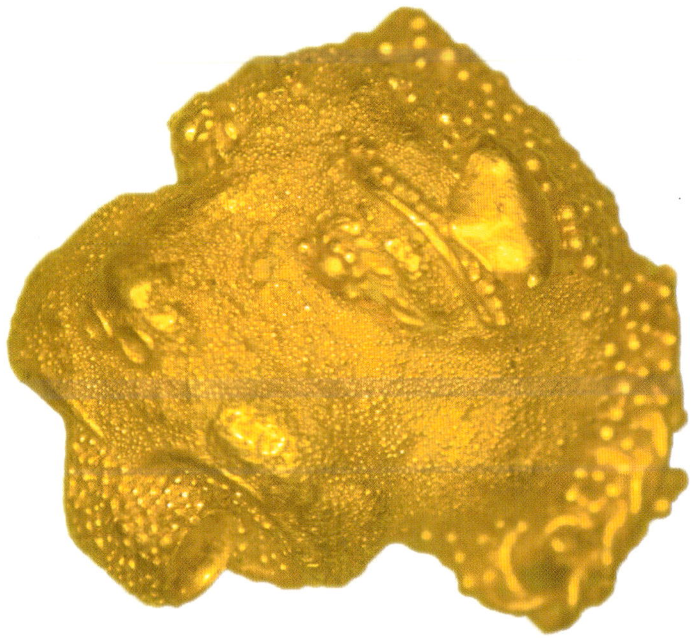

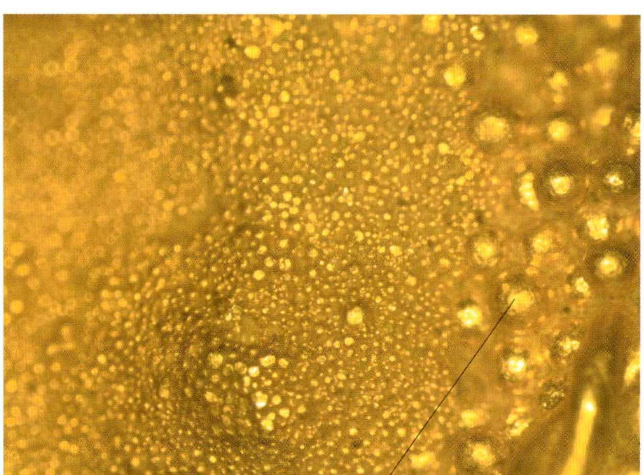

the surface is covered in individual granules

spirals from folding and twisting gold sheet to form wire

Figs. 2.59–2.61 Granulated lion head bead. The bead which is covered in granules of differing sizes shows the possible influence of the Hellinistic world. Bang Kluay Nok in Ranong on the western coast of the peninsula, SuthiRatana Foundation, Bangkok, BKN23, (83.8% gold, 11.5% silver).

GILDING

Because gold can be hammered repeatedly to achieve very thin sheet and leaf without fracturing or cracking, it lends itself to the covering and/or coating of objects made of other materials. Beads produced by simply wrapping hammered gold foil over square shaped clay cores were excavated at the Iron Age cemetery site of Noen U-Loke in the Mun Valley in Northeastern Thailand which dates to the third to fourth centuries CE (Fig. 2.62) (Higham 2014: 239–256) (now stored in the Phimai National Museum). Another burial at the site was of a man wearing silver ear coils covered in gold leaf (Fig. 2.63). A gold-covered silver ear ornament found at the site of Prohear about 65 km east of Phnom Penh and 40 km west of the Vietnamese border dated to between the second century BCE and first century CE, indicates that gold was not confined to covering less expensive materials but was also used to cover other precious metals. In these examples it is not clear whether the gold was burnished onto the silver surfaces with or without the addition of applied heat which would have promoted some solid-state diffusion of the gold with the metal beneath.

The site of Prohear has also produced evidence of another form of gilding, known as depletion gilding, which involves intentionally enriching the surface of low-grade gold alloys (Reinecke 2012, Schlosser, Reinecke, Schwab, Pernicka, Sonetra & Vin Laychour 2012). This is the first time that use of this technique, which was widely used throughout the pre-Colombian world, has been reported in Southeast Asia.

Fig. 2.62 Beads produced by wrapping hammered gold foil over square shaped clay cores were recovered around a women's neck together with agate beads in Burial 113 at Noen U-Loke, Mun Valley, Northeastern Thailand, 3rd–4th centuries CE. Courtesy Charles Higham.

Fig. 2.63 Silver ear coils covered in gold leaf which now appear purple in colour due to the silver chloride corrosion products. Noen U-Loke, Mun Valley, Northeastern Thailand, 3rd–4th centuries CE. Courtesy Charles Higham.

Fig. 2.64 Gold foil inlaid into blue glass bead (now discoloured) found at the Pyu period site of Beikthano BTO-5, Myanmar, Acc No. 1997/6/336.

An early example of gold being inserted into recesses of less expensive materials is a blue glass bead inlaid with gold dots excavated at the Pyu site of Beikthano (Fig. 2.64). The gold was inserted into holes 1mm in diameter drilled into the glass. Glass beads have been recovered from early CE sites with gold foil sandwiched within clear glass (Fig. 2.65), a technique which may have been introduced from the Roman Empire. First-millennium Chinese reports mention people in the Nanchao/Upper Burma area, known as the Gold Teeth people. At the early CE Pyu capital of Halin in Myanmar, farmers found an upper jawbone containing gold inlaid into teeth; they were in the process of removing the gold but the Myanmar collector/scholar U Win Maung of Tampawaddy was able to acquire an intact jawbone (Hudson 2003; Tan 2015:35). The maxilla contained eight teeth which had been filed flat and drilled with a pattern of tiny holes each filled with layers of gold foil, each layer being contact-welded to the layer beneath it (Fig. 2.66).[15]

Fig. 2.65 Glass bead from Khao Nun, southern Myanmar with a layer of gold foil sandwiched within the clear glass.

Throughout historic times and still today (Fig. 2.67–2.70) gold leaf, which is thinner than foil, has been widely used to cover large statues of stone and bronze. Within the Khmer Empire, a subterranean chamber at Jayavarman II's eighth-century Ak Yum temple was found to contain two elephant statues covered in gold leaf (Higham 2001: 58). The roofs of the temples would have originally been covered in gold leaf and the tenth-century temple complex of Jayavarman V was known as *Hemasringagiri,* the mountain with the golden summits. When Zhou Daguan recorded his mission to Angkor in 1296, he wrote that there were towers of gold rising above the surrounding walls and a golden bridge with gilded lions, gold was used to cover the giant stone heads at the gates, and he describes an island with a golden temple which could be Neak Pean, near Preah Khan in the middle of the northern Baray (Bunker oral communication).

Fig. 2.66 Gold foil inlaid into teeth, Halin, Myanmar. Courtesy U-Win Maung & Bob Hudson.

Figs. 2.67–2.68 Making gold leaf in Mandalay.

Figs. 2.69–2.70 Packaging the gold leaf.

Fig 2.71 Author applying gold leaf to a reclining Buddha.

In later periods, mercury gilding, also known as fire gilding, was adopted as the preferred technique since it allowed the application of gold to be further controlled to achieve very thin layers. This had the obvious advantage of minimizing the cost relative to the use of thicker gold foil and the application of a very thin layer of gold did not obscure the decorative details cast or sculpted into the object being gilded. The technique of mercury gilding is based on the fact that mercury and gold combine together to form a pasty liquid which can be applied to baser metals; when the object is heated, the mercury is driven off and the gold is left attached to the surface. The use of this technique is identifiable by analytical methods even when it is not visible, because a small amount of mercury will invariably remain within the gold. Pliny the Elder mentions the technique of cold mercury gilding (Natural history, XXIII, 64–65,100) which involves spreading mercury over the object's surface and then applying the gold leaf which forms an amalgam at the interface between the gold and the object.[16] Mercury gilding is known to have been used in China during the Warring States period in the second half of the first millennium BCE, and the gilded images from Dian Shizhaishan were evidently done by mercury amalgam gilding. However the technique does not appear to have been widely used in Southeast Asia until much later. There is no reference to the technique in Indian sacred or technical texts until the tenth century. Bunker's (2008) chronology suggests that amalgam gilding was introduced from China into Vietnam sometime in the seventh and eighth centuries, from where it reached the Khmer kingdom in the tenth century and the northeast of Thailand under Khmer influence in the eleventh century. It does not appear to have been practised by the Thai until the eighteenth century and this may in part be due to the fact that sacred images were cast from high leaded bronzes, which are difficult to mercury gild because the lead will dissolve into the gold surface and spoil the appearance.[17]

Fig. 2.72 Repeated daily applications of gold leaf onto the Maha Muni Buddha in Mandalay.

1 Until the end of the Iron Age, gold was sometimes placed in the inhumation burials that were found throughout Southeast Asia. By the early centuries CE, these traditional practices had largely been replaced by Indianized burial practices.

2 Pre-Columbian gold objects were regularly sent to London to be melted down into gold bars for the Spanish Crown, and looted material became a major economic stimulus for the Spanish economy. Some of the salvaged material sent to London to be transformed into gold bars was saved by Johnson Matthey Ltd. and was subsequently purchased by the British Museum (Scott 2013).

3 For discussions of these issues see Glover 2015 and Vallard et al. 2015.

4 Majumdar (1986, 158–159) translated *rakta kaladhautam* as gold and *sitatara kaladhautam* as silver, but Daube (2003) has reevaluated the texts and reached a more convincing explanation of *rakta kaladhautam* as red gold and *sitatara kaladhautam* as white gold.

5 Upon analysis of a seven-gram gold ingot from Oc Eo, the protohistoric site in the trans-Bassac region of the Mekong Delta in southern Vietnam, was found to contain 19% silver and 5% copper (Malleret 1962:460, Vo Si Khai 2003).

6 The platinoid inclusions were present in greater concentration in the intentional alloys that had the higher gold content and lower silver content because the concentration of the plationoids originally contained within the alluvial gold become diluted when silver is intentionally added.

7 Indus earth is a saline soil rich in nitre and ammonium salts collected from the Indian river valleys. Used for the patination of zinc-rich bidri ware it would have removed silver. The cupellation with lead would have removed any base metal oxides (Kangle 1960, 2.13.47).

8 Another similar coin with an emperor's head on one side is in Klong Tom museum

9 Pyu tin and lead coins have also been found; a selection is on display in the U Thong National Museum.

10 See Jan Christie (2015) for a discussion of the Borobudur reliefs and evidence of the craftsmen's status.

11 Roman scissors and shears existed, but not the fine tools needed for delicate and accurate cutting of sheet gold components. The elaborate silver scissors used in T'ang times were probably for hair cutting rather than metalworking.

12 The only other known gold plaque of this type was found in a burial context in India (Gupta 1980). While a large number of ringstones (perhaps as many as 60) are recorded from the Punjab, eastwards along the Ganges Valley to Bihar and others are held in major museums and private collections including the Metropolitan Museum of Art, New York and the Los Angeles County Museum, this is the only one known to have been found outside the Indian subcontinent. This attests again to ancient contacts between India and Thailand long predating the establishment of Indian-influenced kingdoms in Southeast Asia. The gold fragments were found in a crumpled state with soil still attached and were gently unfolded. Two associated fragments with animal decoration were found not to belong but the two fragments shown in Figs 2.34 were found to join together. The other associated fragment was that of the foil repousseé ornamentation of interlinked 'S' motif.

13 The technique of granulation is thought to have originated in Mesopotamia in about 2000 BCE from where it traveled to the Mediterranean and then to India and Southeast Asia beyond. Examples of Greek granulation jewellery from the end of the 1st millenium BCE were excavated at Taxila (i.e. modern Pakistan).

14 Although the presence of a central hole in the ringstones would not be practical if the stones were used as moulds.

15 The pain incurred by the drilling must have been considerable and it has been suggested that the earthenware containers found at the site may have been used for distilling alcohol, used as a crude form of anaesthetic (Hudson 2003).

16 Analytical methods based on the detection of mercury cannot readily distinguish between these two techniques.

17 From a conservation point of view the presence of a gold layer on a bronze will cause accelerated corrosion of the underlying bronze due to the large difference in electrochemical potential between the gold and the underlying metal. The gold will be cathodically protected while the copper alloy will be undergo accelerated corrosion causing an increase in volume of the copper alloy, which will eventually push off the gilding.

Fig. 3.1 Examination under the microscope and microphotography used to document the details of manufacture.

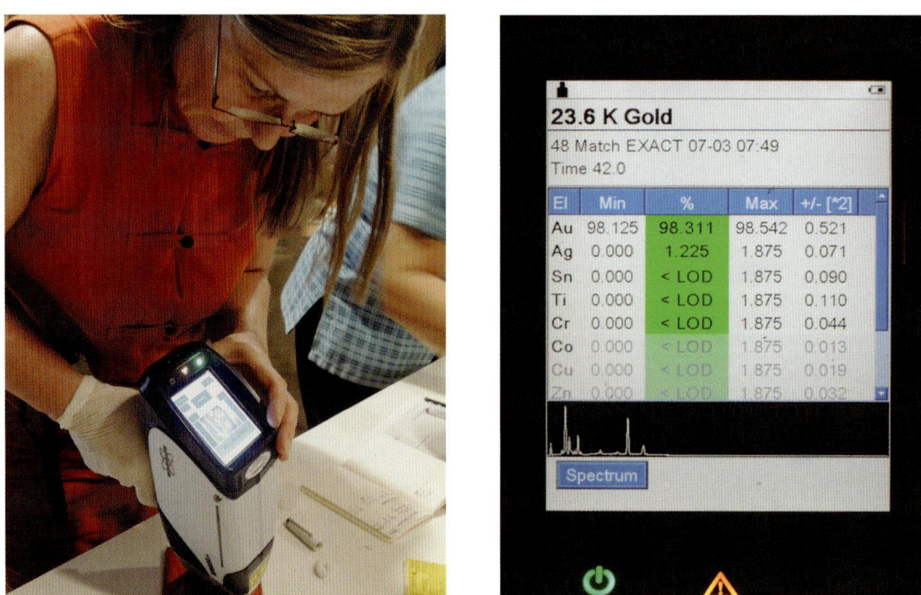

Fig. 3.2 Surface X-ray fluorescence analysis allows non destructive elemental analysis of objects.

CHAPTER 3

CATALOGUE OF GOLD OBJECTS FROM U THONG DVARAVATI PERIOD: 700–1000 CE OR EARLIER

Fig. 3.3 Dvaravati gold objects on display in U Thong National Museum.

SCIENTIFIC EXAMINATION

In a field where there is a lack of settled chronology and a large number of well-made fakes, documentation of the manufacturing techniques provides an objective method of study.

Examination under the microscope helps us develop a picture of an object's history prior to its deposition. If an object was not used or had a purely ritual significance, it will have a very different appearance under the microscope than that of an object, such as the gold seal figs. 1.60–1.63, which was in use over a prolonged period. Jewellery handed down as an heirloom over several generations and deposited for safekeeping, will show a characteristic pattern of random micro scratches, some of which may be quite distinct while others are almost completely worn away (cat. no. 4). The Buddha head, cat. no. 1 showed evidence of repairs and was clearly in circulation over a prolonged period.

Superficial tarnish, which in some cases can be attractive and highly desirable, is referred to as "patina" and can be derived from the deposition of metal ions from ground water, as in the case of the reddish iron staining often apparent on excavated gold surfaces. The presence of such a patina indicates that there have been no recent interventions such as cleaning, and soil deposits may remain deeply embedded within the recesses of the surface, suggesting that the object is in its excavated condition (cat. no. 17). Patinas on gold will almost invariably be extremely thin and can be readily damaged or accidentally removed by injudicious handling.

1. BUDDHA HEAD AND LEG FRAGMENT

Fig. 3.4 Head, foot, leg and miscellaneous sheet gold fragments on display at the National Museum U Thong. Courtesy Phoowadon Duangmee.

The head, the foot and leg were found by the Fine Arts Department of Supanburi during the restoration of chedi no. 2 in 1963 (FAD 2545). They were found at different locations within the sanctuary, the head buried on the terrace in the northwest corner of the chedi, together with the broken *Dharmachakra* (inv. no. 75/2506) displayed in the museum, a stucco Buddha head, terracotta tablets, a terracotta *kinnari* and a fragment of a seated bronze Buddha image. The foot and leg fragment were found beneath the western entrance.

Fig. 3.5 Drawing of chedi no. 2, the find location. FAD 2002.

THE HEAD

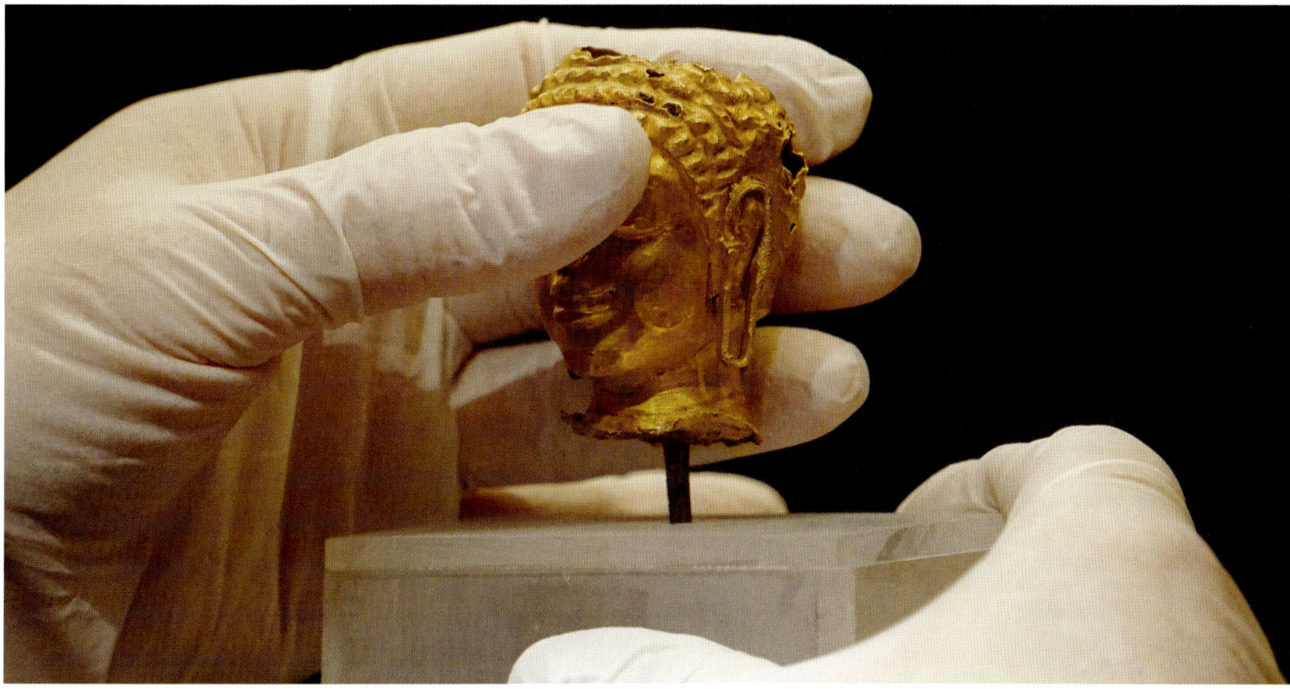

Fig. 3.6 Buddha head being removed from exhibition for examination. Courtesy Phoowadon Duangmee.

Weight: 57.95g including iron armature and soil
Height of head without tang: 55.2 mm
Diameter of neck opening: 38.5 mm
Width: 35.3 mm
Width of left ear: 26.8 mm
Width of right ear: 26.5 mm
MT: 0.54, 0.55 and 0.62 mm
Manufacture: hammered gold sheet over a clay core and iron armature
Elemental composition:
front of forehead: 94.62% gold, 4.57% silver, 0% copper, 0% tin, (0.79% iron from surface contamination)
front of hair: 94.79% gold, 4.38% silver, 0% copper, 0.65% tin
cheek: 95.3% gold, 4.56% silver, 0% copper, 0% tin
back of head: 91.84–95.09% gold, 4.56–5.19% silver, 0% copper, 0.2–0.54% tin
Find location: objects found in 1963 during the restoration of chedi no. 2 U Thong sanctuary by FAD Supanburi. Found on the terrace of the north west corner together with a stucco head, terracotta tablets, a terracotta *kinnari* and a fragment of a *Dharmachakra*
Present location: National Museum U Thong
Inventory number: 10/76/2506 (1953 CE) (previous inventory number 8/2507)

Fig. 3.7 The back of the head with repoussé and punched decoration and torn neck edge.

The head is made of hammered gold sheet over a clay core (Fig. 3.8). The facial features were achieved by simple repoussé (Fig. 3.13) and the details of the hair with the use of a simple punch (Fig. 3.7). The ears were made separately and soldered to the side of the head (Fig. 3.14).

The remains of the original iron armature are visible at the top of the head (Fig. 3.9). A modern replacement tang has been inserted into the neck opening to serve as a mount and can be seen protruding from the neck opening (Fig. 3.8). There are several areas of damage where the gold is missing and the inner core is visible (Fig. 3.9, 3.10), and there is evidence of several attempts of repair (Fig. 3.11). These repairs are themselves covered in patina and wear and do not appear to be modern, suggesting that the object was in circulation over a prolonged period prior to and after the repairs were undertaken. The head was originally attached to another piece of gold which presumably formed the body, and although this is now lost, a small section of the gold sheet is still visible inserted into the head (Fig. 3.12). The neck edge has not been cut or broken accidentally, but rather it was intentionally torn and the head may have existed as a separate object prior to being deposited at the sanctuary.

Fig. 3.8

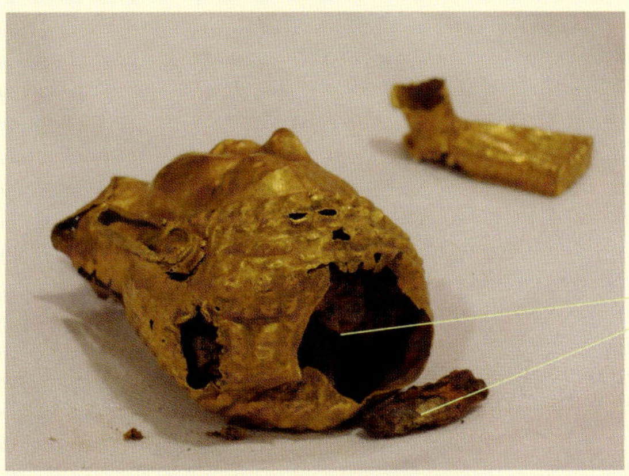

Fig. 3.9

Fig. 3.10

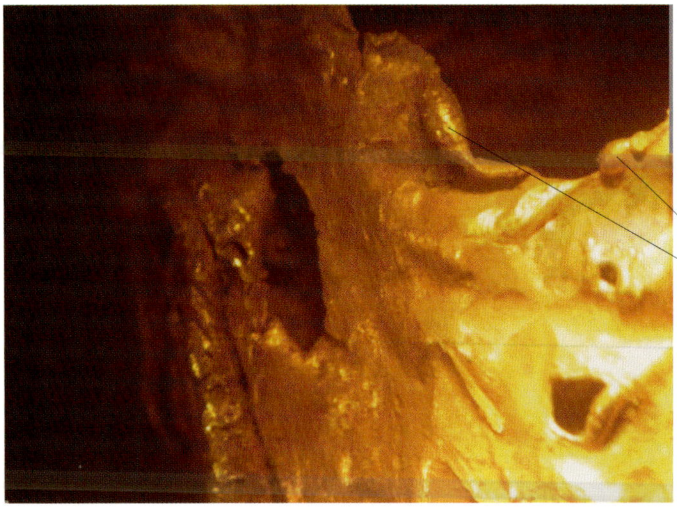

evidence of heating the gold in an attempt to repair a missing area. The surface of the repair shows evidecne of wear.

Fig. 3.11

Fig. 3.12a

a separate gold sheet was inserted into the neck opening

torn neck edge

original clay core

Fig. 3.12b The torn neck edge.

Fig. 3.13 Facial features were achieved by simple repoussé.

Fig. 3.14 The ears were made separately and soldered to the side of the head.

FOOT AND LEG FRAGMENT

87.38% Gold (Au)
11.46% Silver (Ag)
0.69% Tin (Sn)

87.22% Gold (Au)
11.40% Silver (Ag)
0.90% Tin (Sn)

87.54% Gold (Au)
10.80% Silver (Ag)
0.48% Tin (Sn)

Fig. 3.15

Weight of foot: 4.79g
Length: 33.05 mm
Diameter: 15.2 mm
Height: 29.22 mm
MT of foot: 0.54 mm
Weight of leg fragment: 2.76 g including iron armature
Manufacture: foot is hammered gold sheet, the leg fragment is hammered gold sheet over a clay core and iron armature which are still present
Elemental composition:
leg fragment: 87.38% gold, 11.46% silver, 0% copper, 0.69% tin
top of foot: 87.22% gold, 11.4 % silver, 0% copper, 0.9% tin
underside of foot: 87.54% gold, 10.8% silver, 0% copper, 0.48% tin
Find location: excavated in 1953 by FAD Supanburi at Chedi no. 2 U Thong sanctuary. Found beneath the entrance on the west side of the chedi.
Present location: National Museum U Thong
Inventory number: 10/51/2511

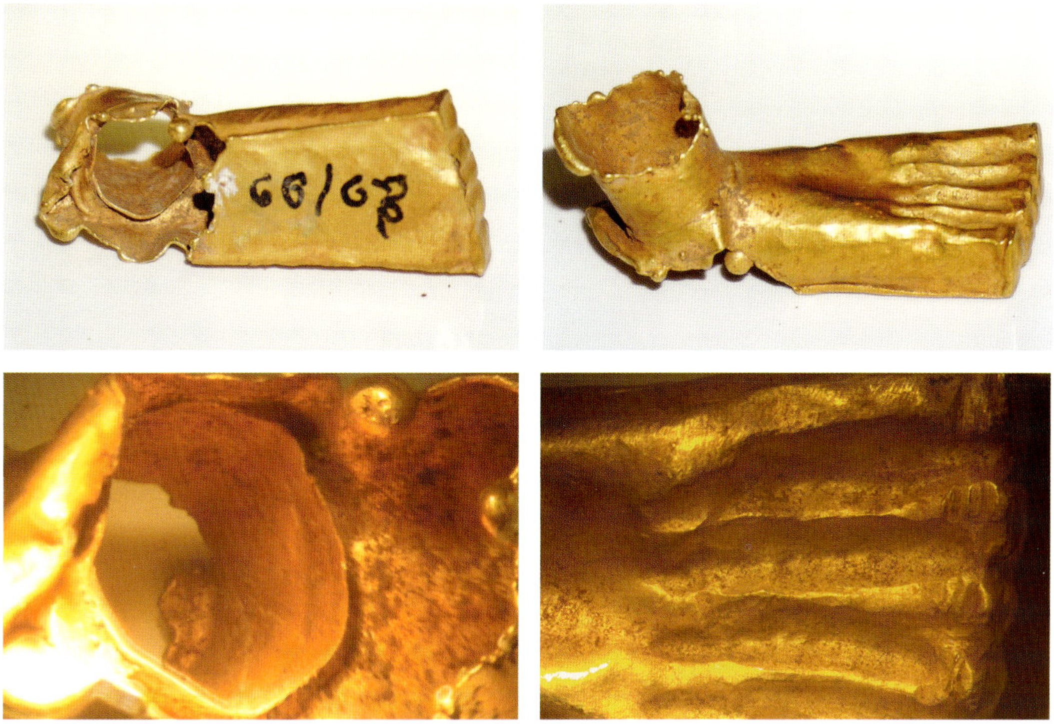

Fig. 3.16 The foot is simply made using several pieces of gold sheet mechanically fitted together. The leg was formed of gold sheet worked over a clay core and iron armature and was attached to the foot by inserting it into the ankle opening. The relief and details of the toes were achieved in repoussé.

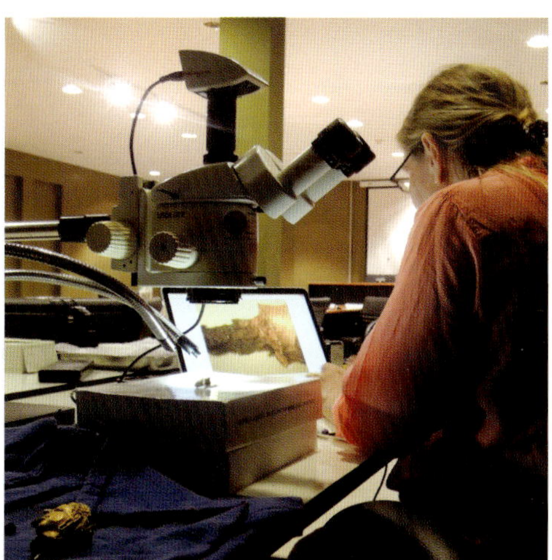

Fig. 3.17 Examining the leg fragment under the microscope.

Fig. 3.18 Leg fragment as seen under the microscope.

ANALYSIS OF THE GOLD COMPOSITION

The gold used for this group undoubtedly came from an alluvial source and there was no attempt to alloy the gold, which was used as found. The high gold concentration would have provided the ideal soft and malleable material for working the gold into thin sheet.

Naturally occurring gold is usually quite pure and is generally associated with silver and copper. Alluvial gold may contain up to 50% silver which is homogeneously distributed within gold but less than 1% copper (in primary deposits the silver concentration ranges between 5 and 40%). The cementation process for separating gold and silver was practiced from the 6th century BCE and involved heating thin sheets of gold with common salt (sodium chloride) at about 800 °C in a sealed clay container for several hours. The salt reacted with the silver to form silver chloride which was volatalised and absorbed into the clay for later recovery, leaving the purified gold (Pliny *Naturalis Historia* 33, 29). Depending on the type of ore used other elements may be associated with the gold. In alluvial gold the association with other alluvial ores such as tin oxide (cassiterite), heavy elements such as platinum and the iron and iron-titanium oxides, the so-called dark sands, may be detected.

A concern in any analysis of ancient gold is the extent of surface change from burial. However, these analyses are all very consistent within the individual parts and the reliability of surface analysis is afforded due to the low levels of copper contained in the alloy, which will have resulted in very minimal surface enrichment. The results can therefore be taken as representative of the whole.
The consistency in the gold composition between the foot 87.2–87.5% gold and 10.8–11.4% silver and the leg 87.4% gold and 11.5% silver suggests that these two pieces were made from the same alluvial gold. There is a significant difference between these analyses and the analyses of the Buddha head which contains less silver 91.9–95.3% gold and 4.4–5.2% silver. It is not possible to extrapolate whether this was simply the result of using different gold but at the same time and place, or whether the objects were made in different workshops and at different times. Separate body parts, such as the foot excavated at Beikthano (Fig. 3.19) were deposited as offerings with no associated material and it is possible that the head and the foot found at Chedi no.2 were not part of the same figure.

PARALLELS:

Pyu Period gold foot found at Beikthano, National Museum, Beikthano, Myanmar, Acc. No. 1980/4/4 (Fig. 3.19)

A gold hand presumed to be Javanese in the Thompson Collection, Yale, inv. No. 2008.21.17 in Miksic: 2011 pl 71, classical period, dimensions: 1.68 x 3 cm 3.73g

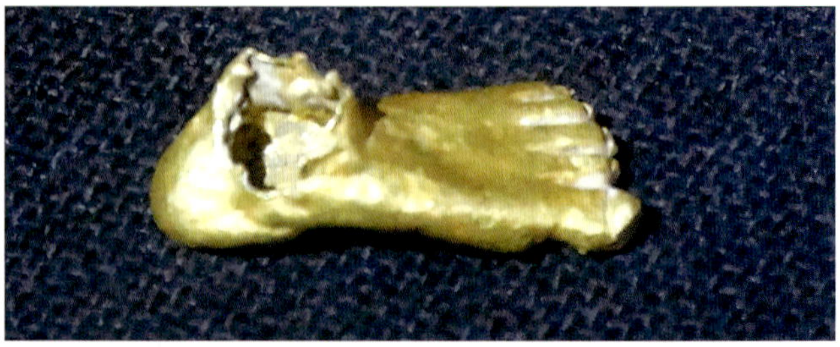

Fig. 3.19 Pyu Period gold foot found at Beikthano, National Museum Beikthano, Myanmar, Acc. No. 1980/4/4.

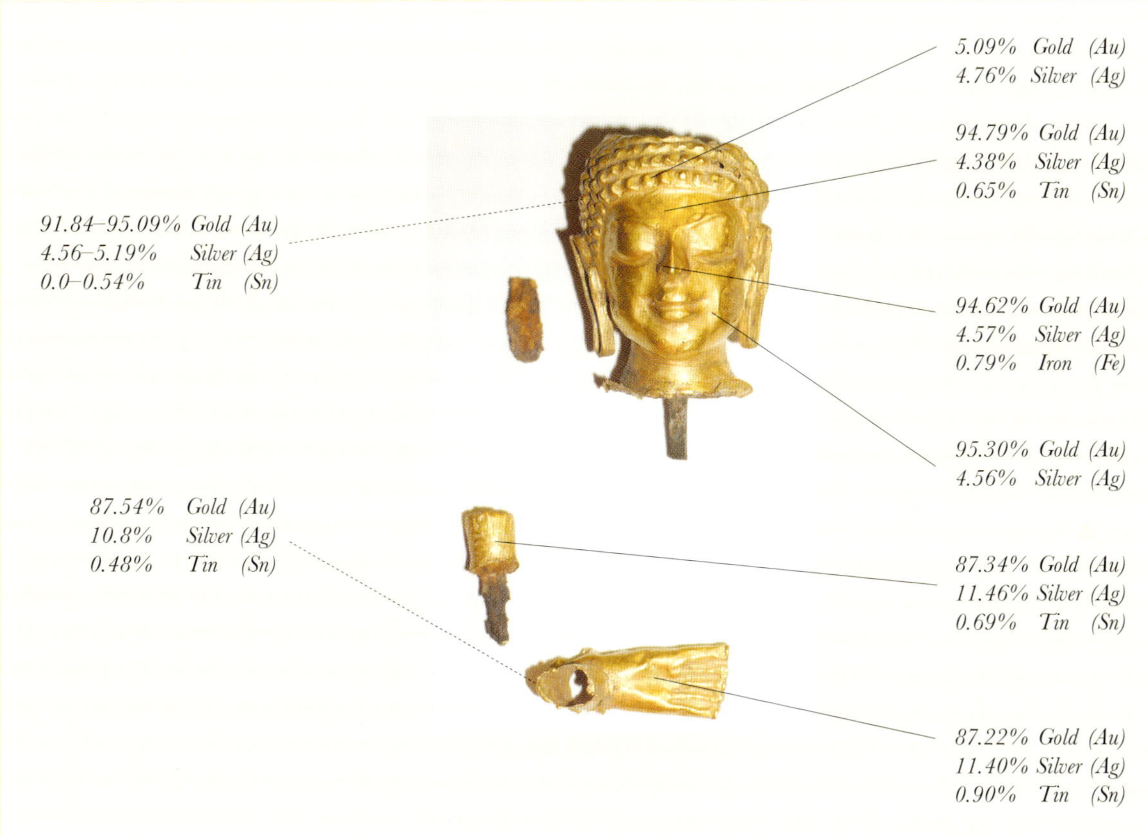

location of analysis	Au	Ag	Cu	Sn	Fe
	%	%	%	%	%
front of forehead	94.62	4.57	0	0	0.79
front of hair	94.79	4.38	0	0.65	
cheek	95.30	4.56	0	0	
back of head	91.84	5.19	0	0.20	
	92.58	5.01	0	0.19	
	95.09	4.76	0	0.11	
	94.40	4.82	0	0.54	
	93.16	4.88	0	0.52	
top of foot	87.22	11.40	nd	0.90	
underside of foot	87.54	10.80	nd	0.48	

Figs. 3.20–3.21 Photograph and table showing the elemental composition of the gold used for the head, the foot and the leg.

2. CASKET LID

Fig. 3.22 © 2016 U Thong National Museum

Weight: not determined
Height: 11.6 mm
Diameter: 27.6 mm
Width: 35.3 mm
MT: 0.48 mm
Manufacture: hammered gold sheet
Elemental composition: not determined
Find location: found at Chedi Wat Pang Yi Sea, U Thong district. The object was found in the grounds of the house belonging to Mr Luan Somboon now built on the site of the chedi. Donated to the museum
Present location: National Museum U Thong
Inventory number: 10/2/2515

PARALLEL: *A bronze example was excavated from Context 46 at Ban Don Ta Phet.*

3. MISCELLANEOUS SQUASHED FRAGMENTS

Fig. 3.23 These fragments require examination in order to determine their original shape and whether they were deposited as fragments or were damaged during burial.

4. GOLD PENDANT AND BEAD NECKLACE

Fig. 3.24 The pendant and beads were not found together but have been assembled for display purposes. © 2016 U Thong National Museum

Weight of pendant and beads: 15.65g
Length of necklace as displayed including beads and pendant: 186 mm
Diameter of pendant: 42.69 mm
Condition: complete and in very good condition
Evidence of use: evidence of wear over the surface of the pendant
Find location: the beads and the pendant were found at different times in U Thong district. The pendant was donated to the museum by Khun Puang Ranksi in 2503. The beads were bough by the FAD in December 2513 from Mr Prasar Thonchuang
Present location: National Museum U Thong
Inventory number of pendant : 10/88/2503 (1960 CE)
Inventory number of beads : 10/2/2513 (1970 CE)

GOLD PENDANT

ANALYSIS OF THE GOLD COMPOSITION

Figs. 3.25–3.26 The decorative motif on the pendant might allude to the *Dharmachakra*. The pendant was hammered from gold sheet with 81–82% gold, 16. 5% silver, 1–1.5% copper and 0.5% tin, 10/88/2503.

Front		
81.12%	Gold	(Au)
16.34%	Silver	(Ag)
1.38%	Copper	(Cu)
0.47%	Tin	(Sn)

Reverse		
81.86%	Gold	(Au)
16.54%	Silver	(Ag)
1.09%	Copper	(Cu)
0.50%	Tin	(Sn)

Diameter of pendant: 42.69 mm
Manufacture of pendant: probably hammered into a stone mould such as the one in Fig. 2.3. The stone inlay (not identified) in the centre of the pendant appears to be original and is mechanically held in place by crimping the surrounding gold. The suspension loop was made of a strip of gold sheet which was soldered to the top of the reverse of the pendant and simply folded over on itself
Elemental composition:
Front: 81.12% gold, 16.34% silver, 1.38% copper, 0.47% tin
Back: 81.86% gold, 16.54% silver, 1.09% copper, 0.50% tin
Condition: complete and in very good condition
Evidence of use: evidence of wear over the surface

PARALLELS:

Fig. 3.27 Hammered gold sheet, Lopburi chance find.

Fig. 3.28 Gold sheet hammered into a mould with a central pierced hole from Ratch Buri. Diameter: 13 mm, RBR 149.

Fig. 3.29 Thin hammered gold sheet, Musée Guimet, Paris.

5. THREE TYPES OF GOLD BEAD

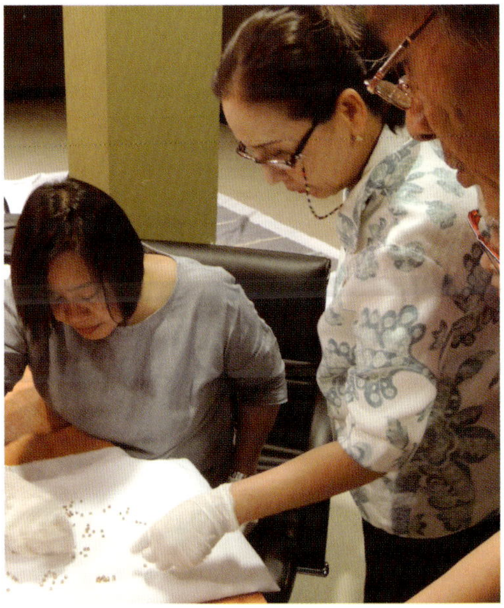

Figs. 3.30–3.31 The director of U Thong National Museum Khun Dendao Siilapanon and the museum staff dismantle the necklace to facilitate examination.

Fig. 3.32 The necklace was made up of three different types of bead.

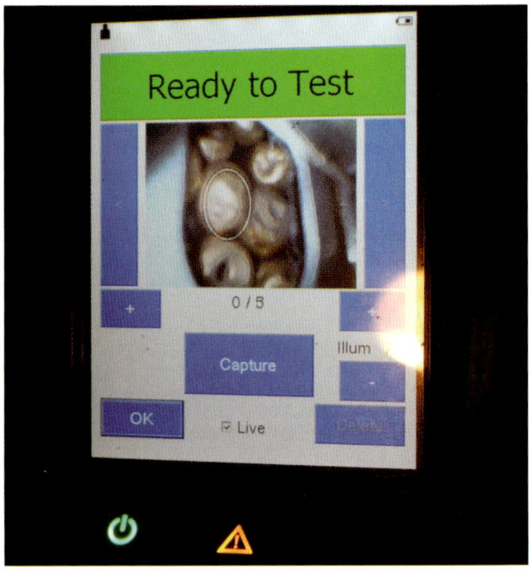

Fig. 3.33 The image of the area being analyzsed is displayed on the screen of the X-ray fluorescence analyzer allowing adjustments in the positioning of the beam.

OCTAGONAL BEAD

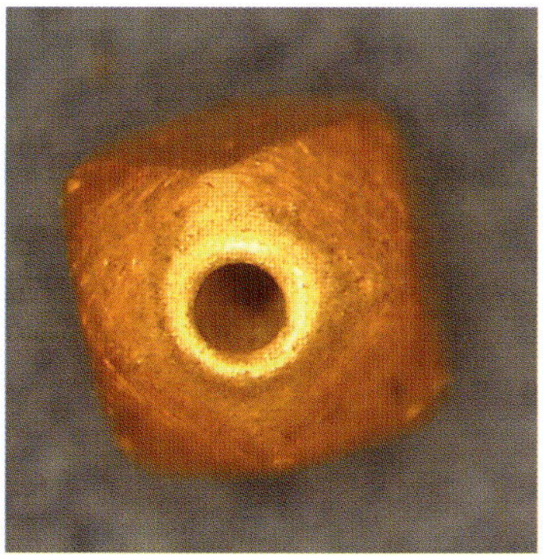

Figs. 3.35, 3.36 Octagonal bead made of hammered sheet over a clay core.

Weight: 0.12 g
Diameter: 3.83 mm
Manufacture: hammered sheet over a clay core
Elemental composition: 94.17% gold, 3.47% silver, 0% copper, 0% tin

ROUND BEAD

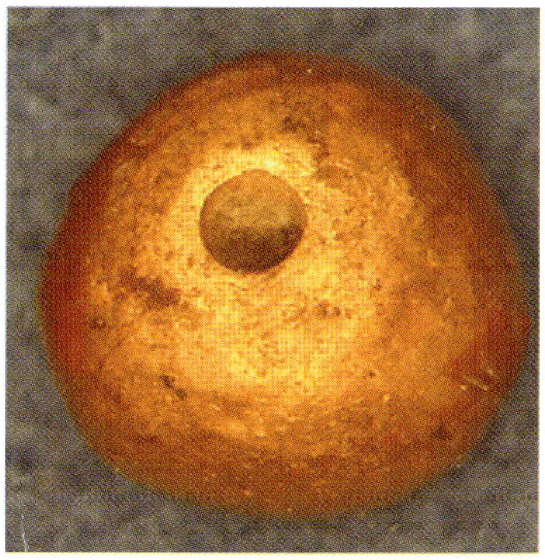

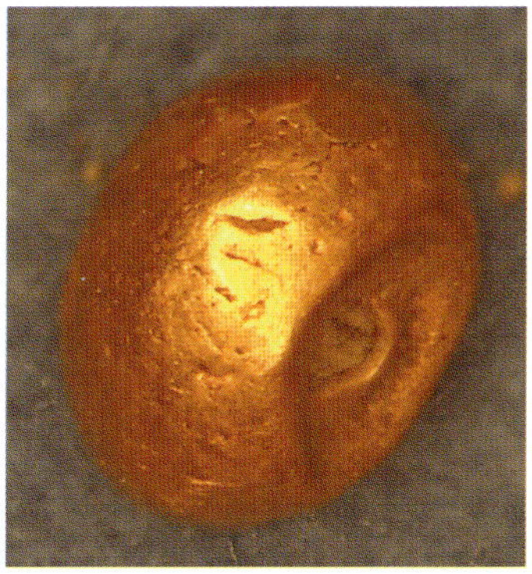

Figs. 3.37, 3.38 Round bead made of hammered sheet over a clay core.

Weight: 0.10 g
Diameter: 4.85 mm
Manufacture: hammered sheet over a clay core
Elemental composition: 82.65% gold, 14.86% silver, 1.16% copper, 0% tin

FACETTED BEAD

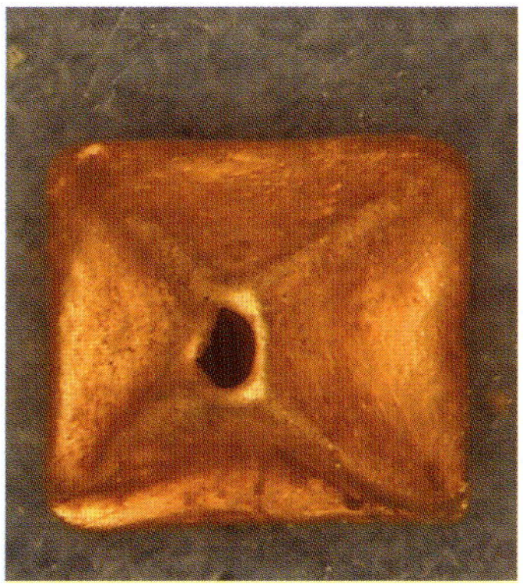

Figs. 3.39, 3.40 Facetted bead made of hammered sheet over a clay core.

Weight: 0.08 g
Diameter: 4.8 mm
Manufacture: hammered sheet over a clay core
Elemental composition: 87.9% gold, 9.4% silver, 2.3% copper, 0% tin

6. SINGLE GOLD BEAD

Fig. 3.41 Bead made of hammered sheet over a clay core.

Manufacture: hammered sheet gold over a clay core. The gold sheet was in two halves which were crimped together (MT 0.15 mm)
Elemental composition: 70% gold, 30% silver,
Find location: Ban Nongong
Present location: donated to the U Thong National Museum by Khun Noi
Inventory number: 10/002/2558

Figs. 3.42 Hammered sheet gold over a clay core. Thickness of gold 0.15 mm.

Figs. 3.43–3.45 The gold sheet was in two halves which were crimped together around the centre of the bead.

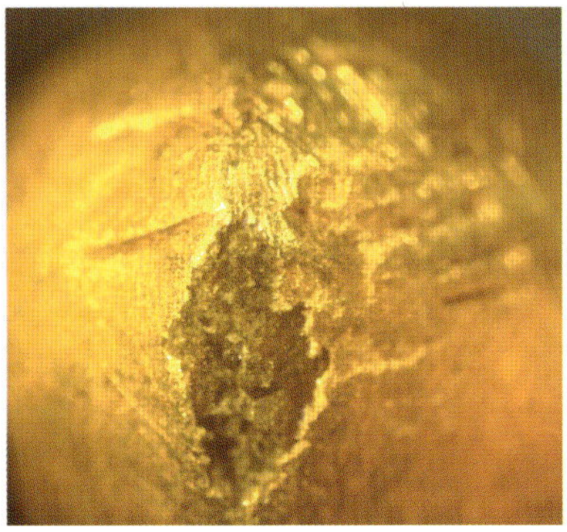

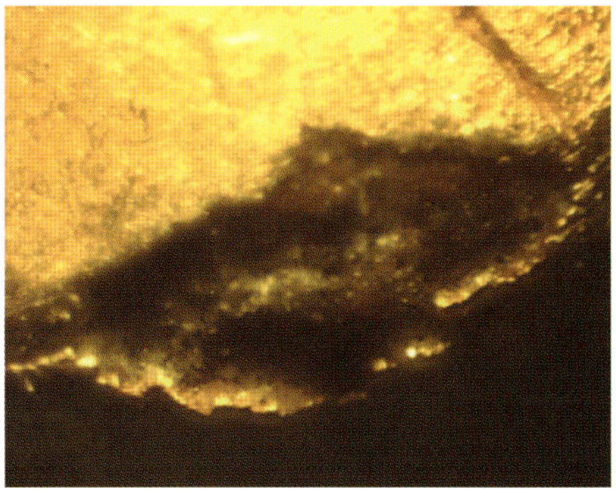

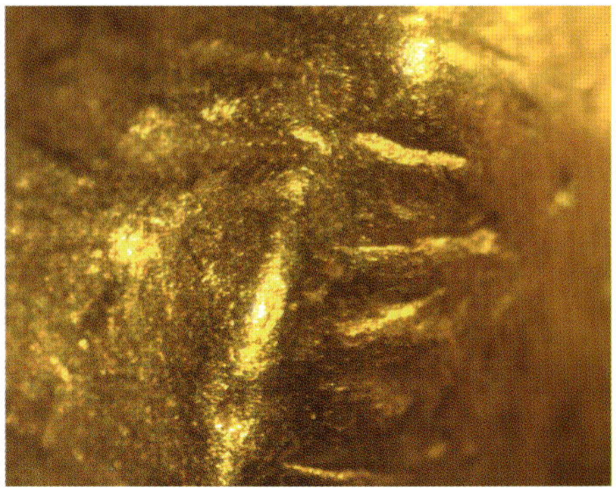

7. HEAVY SPLIT-RING HINGED EAR ORNAMENT

Fig. 3.46 © 2016 U Thong National Museum

Weight: 26.11g
Weight of half without tang: 12.27 g
Weight of half with tang: 13.86 g
Height: 19.7 mm
Diameter: 20.4 mm
Manufacture: cast in a two piece mould
Elemental composition:
half without tang 98.76% gold, 1.15% silver, 0% copper, 0.0% tin
half with tang 98.31% gold, 1.22% silver, 0% copper, 0.0% tin
Find location: found accidentally in museum compound
Present location: U Thong National Museum
Inventory number: 10/001/2553

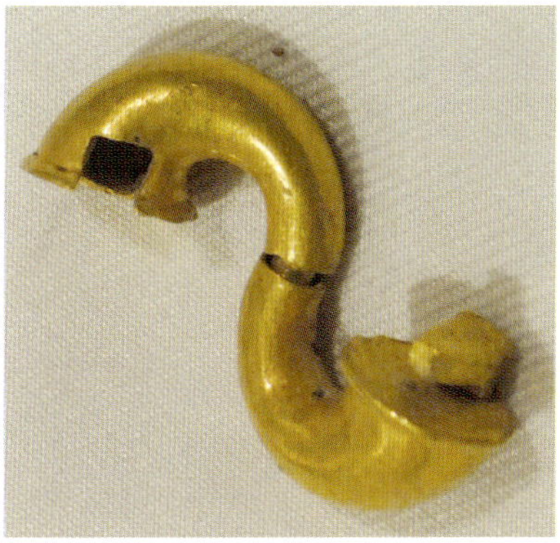

Figs. 3.47–3.49 The ear ornament is hinged at the top centre.

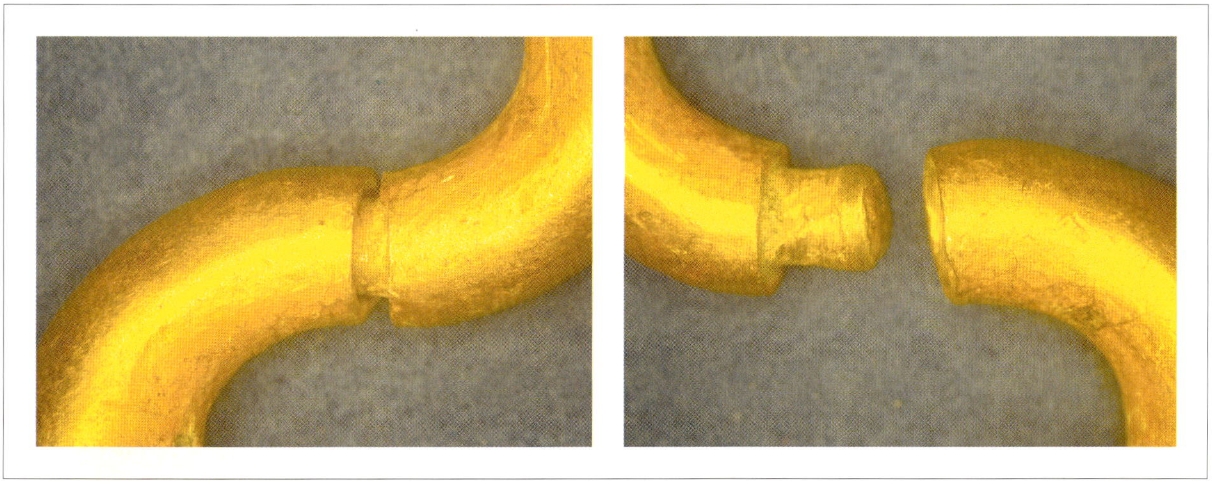

Fig. 3.50–3.51 Detail of the hinge which allowed the ear ornament to be closed after it was inserted into the ear lobeThis suggests domestic use rather than use as an ornament for temple sculpture.

Fig. 3.52 The analysis indicates that the object was cast in a high gold content unalloyed gold.

Figs. 3.53–3.55 Details of the fixing mechanism.

MANUFACTURE

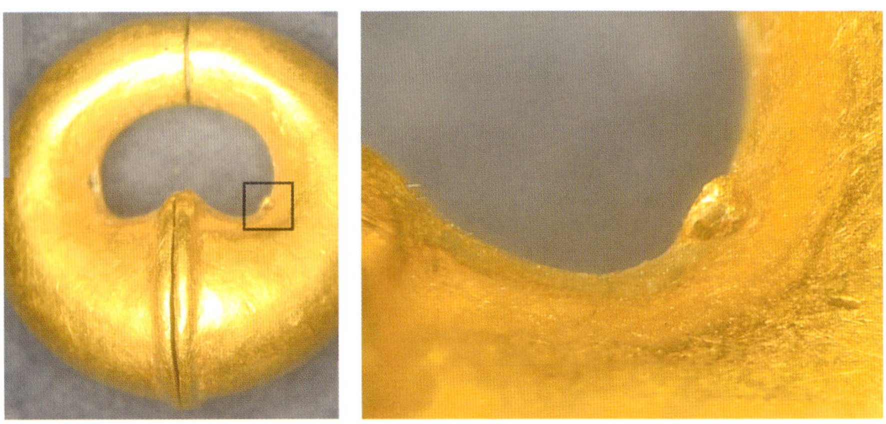

Fig. 3.56 The object was cast. Small depressions on the internal edge may have secured the ornament during the casting process.

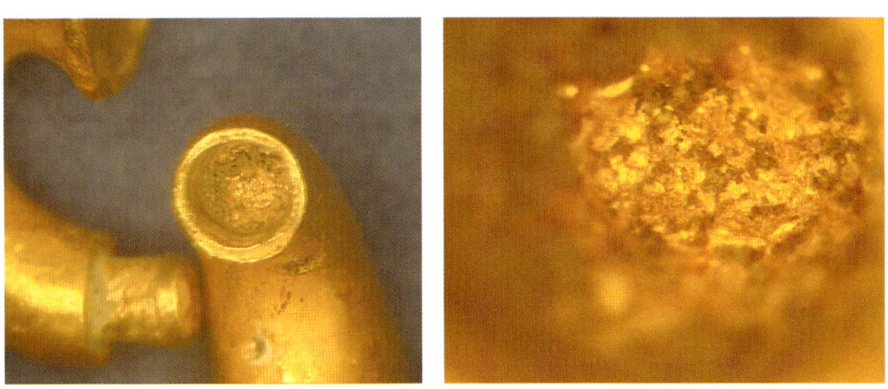

Figs. 3.57–3.58 The cast texture of the gold surface is visible within the hinge mechanism.

PARALLELS:

Fig. 3.59 Hinged ear ornament, illustrated in Richter 2000: 89 Pls 78 and 79, no provenance given.

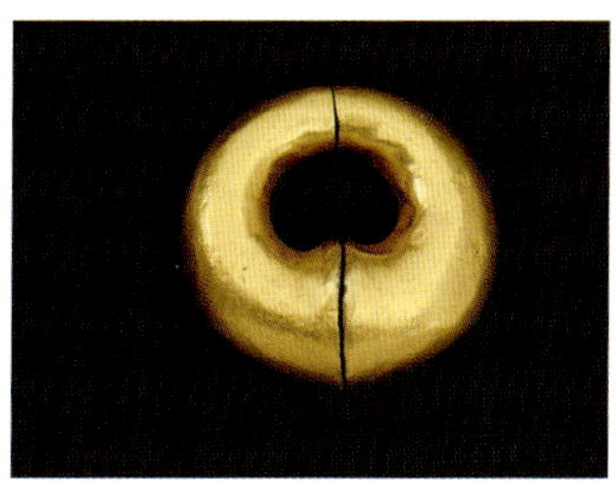

Fig. 3.60 Hinged ear ornaments Yale 2007.142.162 in Miksic 2011: 174 Pl 49 Classical period, dimensions: 2.27 x 2.27 cm, 27.05 g. Courtesy Yale University Art Gallery. *Fig. 3.61* Hinged ear ornament, Ghysels private collection Brussels, in von Custom 2001: 257.

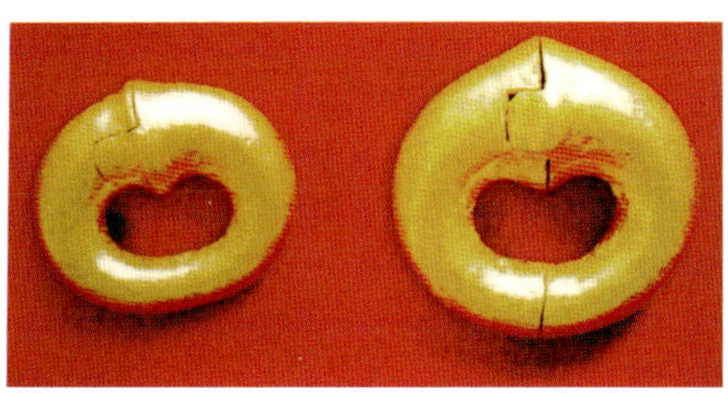

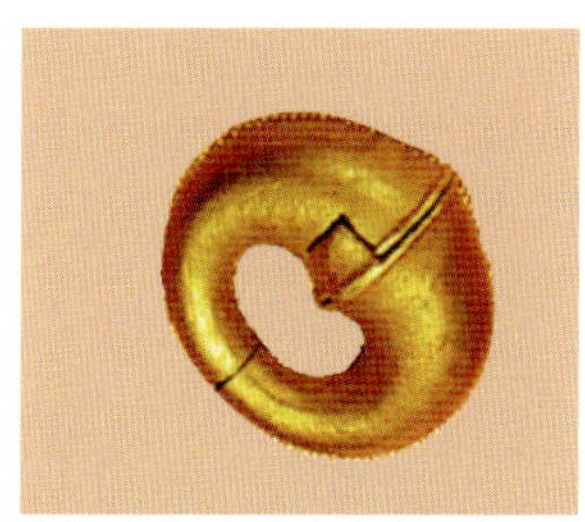

Figs. 3.62–3.63 Hinged ear ornaments found at Oc Eo, Miksic 2003 Pl 1.2; Richter 2000: 39 Pl 33.

These hinged types of ear ornament are quite rare but an almost identical one was excavated at the ancient port site of Oc Eo in southern Vietnam, dated to the second to the fifth CE (Miksic 2003 Pl. 1.2 and Richter 2000 Pl. 33). Other Javanese examples dated to the Classic Period are on display at Yale University Museum (Miksic 2011 Pl. 49) and in the Ghysels collection, Brussels (von Custom 2001:257).

The more usual type of split ear ornament is found over widespread areas in Southeast Asia and is shown on the Dvaravati period terracotta friezes and in moulds for casting found at U Thong and now displayed in the U Thong National Museum (Figs. 2.31, 2.38, 3.71).

Fig. 3.64 Stone moulds used for casting the more usual unhinged type of split ear ornament.

Fig. 3.65 Terracotta relief depicting a male dancer showing the dress and elaborate jewellery worn at this period, National Museum U Thong, 10/29/2543. Baptiste and Zéphir 2009. Courtesy Guimet Museum.

Fig. 3.66 The more usual type of split ear ornament depicted on Dvaravati period sculpture, U Thong National Museum, 30/2543, 1/24, 2002/2518. Courtesy Musée Guimet.

Fig. 3.67 Lopburi National Museum, 2003–2004/2518 2007/2518. Courtesy Musée Guimet.

8. FIGURE OF A *KINNARI*

The Hindu-Buddhist celestial musician in which bird and human elements are combined.

Fig. 3.68 The figure is made by repoussé with additional detail chased into the gold surface. A supporting backplate has been attached to the reverse of the figure and a wire loop has been soldered onto the base which would have allowed the object to be worn (width of wire: 1.9 mm). © 2016 U Thong National Museum

Weight: 2.87g
Height: 18.89 mm
Width: 12.4 mm
Manufacture: made in three sections. The front is made by repoussé with chased detail. A supporting backplate is attached to the reverse of the figure and a wire loop attachment has been soldered onto the base allowing the ornament to be worn (width of wire: 1.9 mm)
Elemental composition: 87.1% gold, 16.15% silver, 0.96% copper, 0% tin
Find location: U Thong ancient city
Present location: U Thong National Museum
Inventory number: 10/275/2509 (1956 CE)

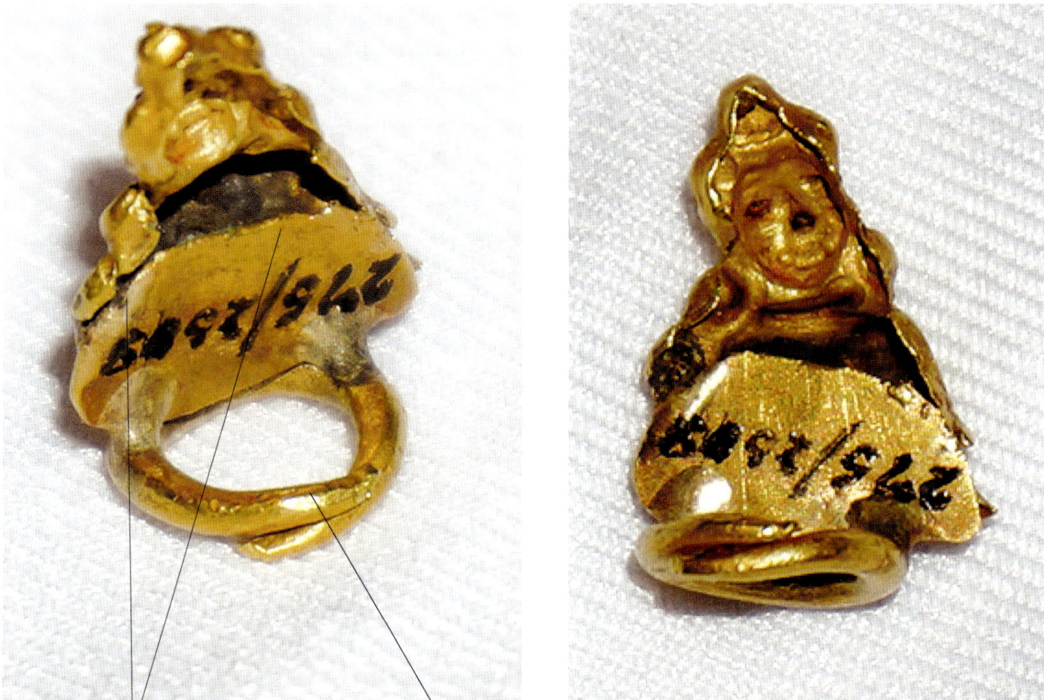

Figs. 3.69–3.70 Reverse of the figure showing the supporting backplate and the gold wire attachment. The presence of the loop soldered onto the base of the figure indicates that it was intended to be worn and appears to have been adapted after its original manufacture.

Fig. 3.71 Front of figure showing the join with the backplate and the soldered base.

Fig. 3.72 Ear ornament, presumed to be Javanese. Like the U Thong example it has an attachment on the reverse which would have enabled it to be worn. This example appears to be cast in the round. Yale 2007.142.195 in Miksic 2011:187 Pl 58, Classical period, dimensions: 1.5 x 1.05 cm 3.91 g. Courtesy Yale University Art Gallery.

Fig. 3.73 Ear ornament, presumed to be Javanese. Richter 2000, no provenance given.

9. EAR ORNAMENT IN THE REPRESENTATION OF THE FACE OF *KIRTIMUKHA*

The famished demon who emerged from the head of Shiva.

Figs. 3.74–3.75 Ornament cast with much of the detail achieved in the casting. There was some further enhancing of the detail after casting and a feathering pattern visible around the mouth of the *Kirtimukha* is due to the use of a straight edged tool being employed to chase around corners. An attachment soldered onto the reverse allowed the object to be worn.

Weight: 4.57 g
Height: 18.8 mm
Width: 10.7 mm
Elemental composition: 72.25% gold, 19.07% silver, 0% copper, 0% tin, some soil contamination
Manufacture: cast gold, with some subsequent chasing. A slight feathering is visible around the mouth due to the use of a straight edged tool to chase around corners. The attachment ring on the reverse is soldered on
Condition: complete
Evidence of use: no
Find location: unknown, register only says it was found in U Thong
Present location: U Thong National Museum
Inv. no. 10/274/2509

10. EAR CLIP WITH STONE INLAY

Figs. 3.76–3.77 This type of small ear ornament is sometimes described as a bird ring used on the legs of pet birds. However, there is no evidence for this and it is perhaps more likely that they were fitted to the upper helix of the ear. This example appears to be a composite made up from separate elements which were not originally intended to fit together.

Weight: 4.29 g
Height: 22.5 mm
Diameter of ring: 12.9 mm
Elemental composition: 92.1% gold, 6.5% silver
Manufacture: hammered sheet and beaded wire soldered together
Condition: damaged and slightly misshapen, the stone is loose in its setting and no longer in the correct place. The stone appears light green from the reverse which has largely been protected but grey from the front due to weathering
Evidence of use: worn
Find location: unknown, register only says it was found in U Thong
Present location: U Thong National Museum
Inv. no. 10/280/2509

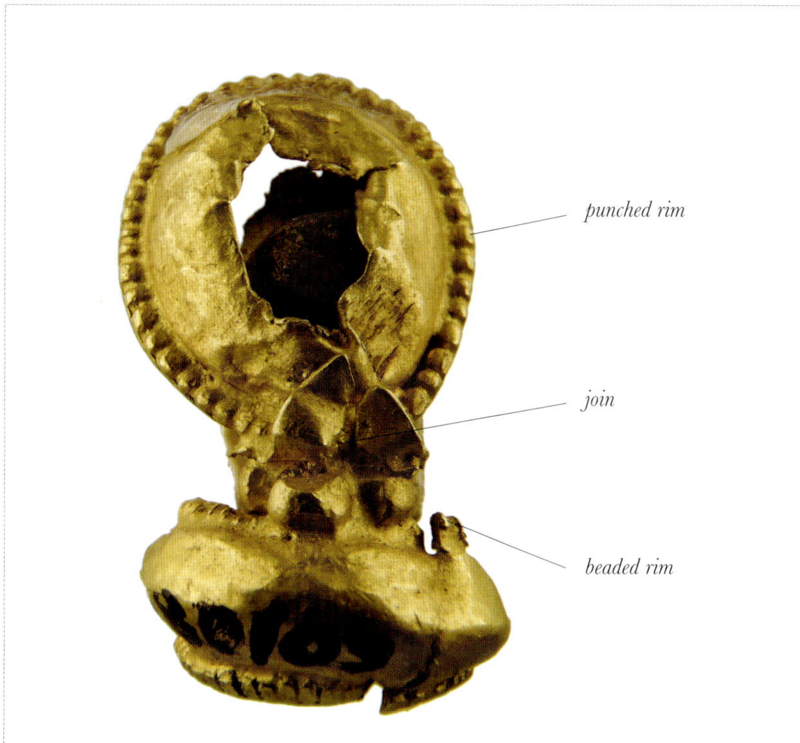

Fig. 3.78 The object is made in two parts which are clumsily fitted together. A join is clearly visible between the upper gold mount and the base of the ear clip; the decorated rim on the ear clip is made of beaded wire; this is not the same as the rim on the stone mount which is punched to simulate beaded wire. The two parts may not have originally belonged together. © 2016 U Thong National Museum

PARALLELS:

Fig. 3.79 Bird rings in Miksic 2011:Pl 43 Javanese, Classical period. Courtesy Yale University Art Gallery.

11. EAR ORNAMENT

Fig. 3.80 © 2016 U Thong National Museum

Fig. 3.81

Weight: 1.96 g
Width: 12.17 mm
Elemental composition: not determined
Manufacture: hammered gold bar with added granualtion
Condition: complete
Evidence of use: no
Find location: unknown, register only says it was found in U Thong
Present location: U Thong National Museum
Inventory number: 10/278/2509

12. PLAIN WIRE RING

Fig. 3.82 © 2016 U Thong National Museum

Weight: 1.16 g
Width: 9.73 mm
Elemental composition: not determined
Manufacture: hammered
Condition: complete
Evidence of use: no
Find location: unknown, register only says it was found in U Thong
Present location: U Thong National Museum
Inventory number: 10/277/2509

13. EAR ORNAMENT WITH A PYRAMID DROP AND GRANULATION

Fig. 3.83 © 2016 U Thong National Museum

Weight: 1.31 g
Diameter: 8.13 mm
Diameter bead: 4.97 mm
Manufacture: hammered gold wire and granulation
Condition: complete
Evidence of use: unclear
Find location: chance find U Thong
Present location: U Thong National Museum
Inventory number: 10/279/2509

14. EAR ORNAMENT WITH DROP

Fig. 3.84 © 2016 U Thong National Museum

Weight: 0.95 g
Height: 18.62 mm
Height of drop: 8.85 mm
Diameter drop: 7.13 mm
Manufacture: drop possibly cast and gold wire hammered
Condition: drop squashed
Evidence of use: unclear
Find location: chance find U Thong
Present location: UThong National Museum
Inventory number: 10/276/2509

15. AGATE STONE AMULET WITH GOLD MOUNTS

Fig. 3.85

Weight: 0.95 g
Height: 18.62
Manufacture: two strips of gold sheet used to repair the stone. Holes were punched through the gold and a gold pin inserted through drilled holes in the stone
Find location: chance find U Thong
Present location: U Thong National Museum
Inventory number: -

16. GROUP OF FINGER RINGS WITH STONES

Fig. 3.86 Inventory number: 10/282/169
© 2016 U Thong National Museum

Weight: 0.96 g
Diameter: 16.25 mm
Manufacture: hammered gold ring, separate mount with beaded wire soldered on
Condition: stone missing
Find location: chance find U Thong
Present location: U Thong National Museum

Fig. 3.87 Inventory number: 10/283/63
© 2016 U Thong National Museum

Weight: 1.29 g
Diameter: 18.93 mm
Manufacture: cast
Condition: very worn
Find location: chance find U Thong
Present location: U Thong National Museum

Fig. 3.88 Inventory number: 10/284/09
© 2016 U Thong National Museum

Weight: 2.93 g
Diameter: not determined
Manufacture: cast shank and hammered mount, the ring may have been adapted at a later time
Condition: very worn
Find location: chance find U Thong
Present location: U Thong National Museum

Fig. 3.89 Inventory number: 10/285/09

Weight: 0.94 g
Diameter: 18.0 mm
Manufacture: hammered or cast
Find location: chance find U Thong
Present location: U Thong National Museum

Fig. 3.90 Inventory number: 10/286/03

Weight: 0.67 g
Diameter: 13.4 mm
Manufacture: hammered or cast
Find location: chance find U Thong
Present location: U Thong National Museum

Fig. 3.91 Inventory number: 10/287/03

Weight: 1.25 g
Diameter: 20.9 mm
Manufacture: hammered or cast
Find location: chance find U Thong
Present location: U Thong National Museum

Fig. 3.92 Inventory number: 10/296/2509
© 2016 U Thong National Museum

Weight: 2.28 g
Diameter: 18.1 mm
Manufacture: cast with mount added separately, stone still <u>in situ</u>
Find location: chance find U Thong
Present location: U Thong National Museum

Fig. 3.93 Inventory number: 10/295/2503
© 2016 U Thong National Museum

Weight: 1.35 g
Diameter: 18.7 mm
Manufacture: copper ring with gold mount, stone still <u>in situ</u>
Find location: chance find U Thong
Present location: U Thong National Museum

Fig. 3.94 Inventory number: 10/294/2509
© 2016 U Thong National Museum

Weight: 2.01g
Diameter: 21.8 mm
Manufacture: copper ring with gold mount
Find location: chance find U Thong
Present location: U Thong National Museum

Fig. 3.95 Inventory number: 10/293/2509
© 2016 U Thong National Museum

Weight: 2.73 g
Diameter: 21.7 mm
Manufacture:
Find location: chance find U Thong
Present location: U Thong National Museum

DVARAVATI GOLD OBJECTS FROM UTHONG IN THE SURIYA SURAPANICH COLLECTION

Figs. 3.96–3.97 Suriya Surapanich and their collection.

17. SPLIT RING EAR ORNAMENT WITH GRANULATED DECORATION

Figs. 3.98–3.99 The exterior is almost entirely covered with granulation.

Weight: 4.30 g
Diameter: 21.56 mm
Height: 20.94 mm
Elemental composition: 71.86% gold, 26.81% silver, 0.0% copper, 0.76% tin, 0.45% Iron from soil contamination
Manufacture: plain hollow gold ear ornament with added granulation
Condition: very good, single small tear from outer edge through to inner edge
Evidence of use: unclear
Find location: corn field, U Thong district
Present location: Suriya Surapanich collection, U Thong

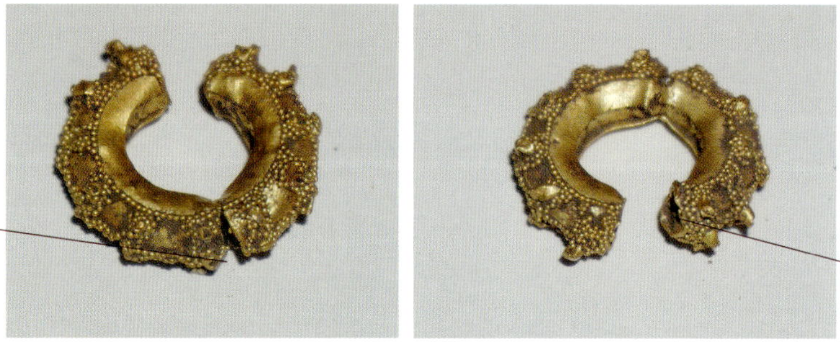

single small tear

hollow

Figs. 3.100–3.101

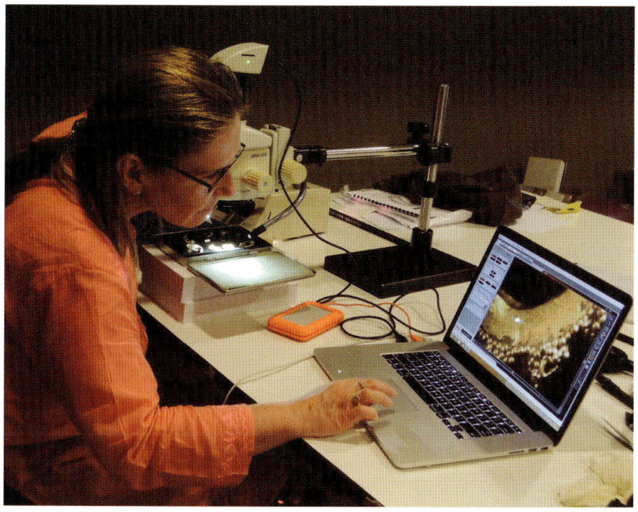

The ear ornament is hollow with a convex profile on the exterior and concave on the interior. The exterior portion is almost entirely covered with granulation. The gold balls were each individually added to the surface to achieve a complex geometric pattern which forms a type of netting effect over the outer surface. There is a single line of granules on the shoulders of the ornament and diamond shaped clusters around a larger hollow ball within the central zone. Examination under the microscope indicates that the work was exceptionally fine, the goldsmith having the technical ability to ensure a calibrated and even size of granule over the entire decorative scheme.

Figs. 3.102–3.103 Ear ornament as seen under the microscope.

Figs. 3.104 showing the very fine workmanship and the burial soil which gave rise to the iron reading on the XRF analysis.

PARALLEL:

Fig. 3.105 Granulated ear ornament, presumed to be Javanese. Yale 2007.142.142 in Miksic 2011:169 Pl 46 Classical period, dimensions: 1.58 x 1.52 cm 2.57 g. Courtesy Yale University Art Gallery.

18. SPLIT RING EAR ORNAMENT
HAIR RING OR GARMENT TOGGLE WITH LARGE GRANULES

Figs. 3.106–3.107

Weight: 4.55 g
Diameter: 14.4 mm
Height: 13.99 mm
Elemental composition: 87.44% gold, 9.37% silver, 0.94% copper, 0% tin,
Manufacture: fused gold wires with granulation decoration
Condition: very good
Evidence of use: unclear
Find location: unknown
Present location: Suriya Surapanich collection, U Thong

Fig. 3.108

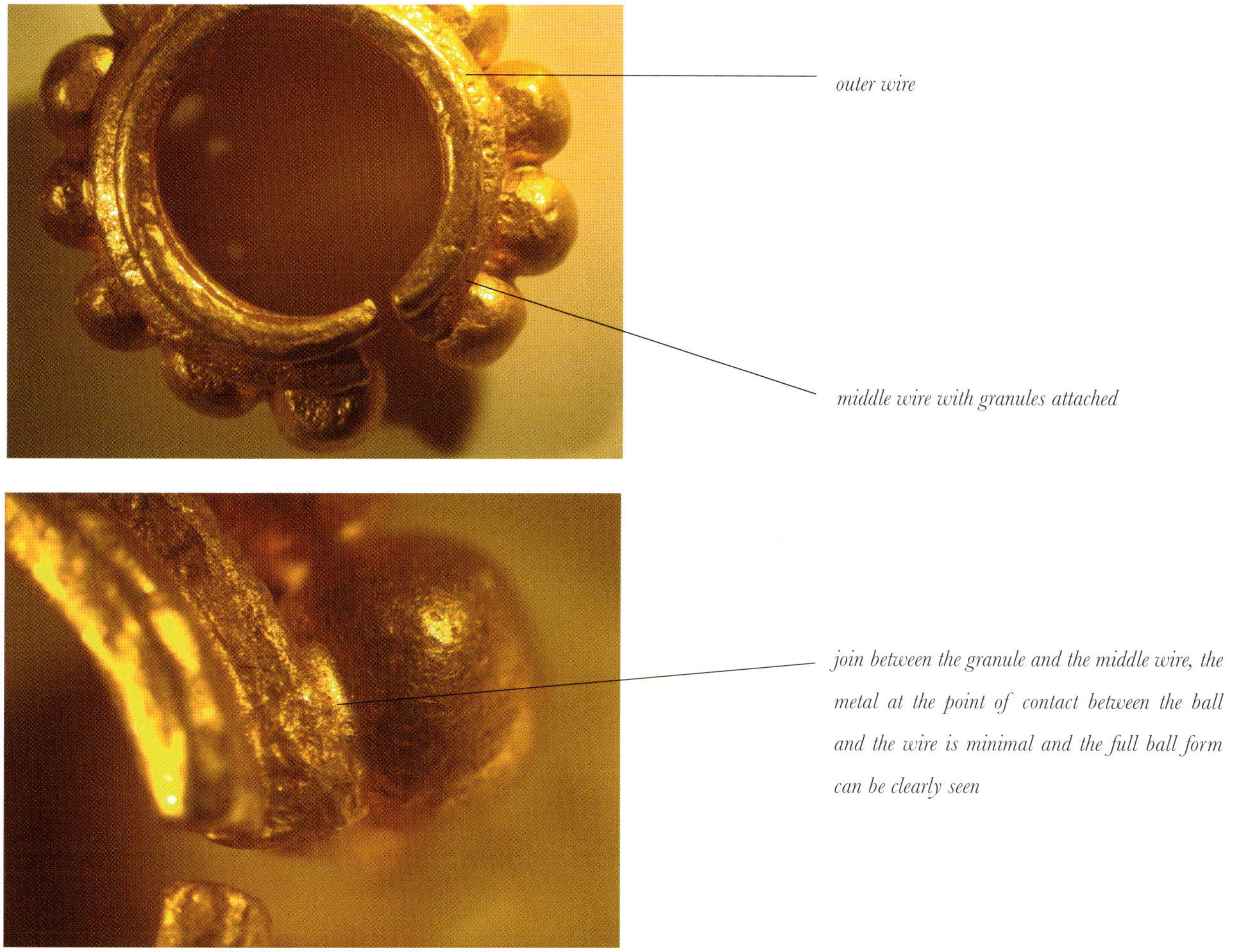

Figs. 3.109–3.110 The ear ornament is composed of three thick gold wires with small balls of gold applied to the outer surface of the middle wire using the technique of granulation. The wires on either side of the central decorated wire are each made up of two thin wires fused together.

Objects such as these have been described as ear ornaments but they might be better suited as cord fasteners such as the numerous cords around the waists of figures depicted on Dvaravati sculpture (Figs. 1.3 & 3.65). Their weight would have ensured that the cord hung vertically. It has also been suggested that these type of ornaments were hair rings as used by the ancient Egyptians.

PARALLELS:

Fig. 3.111 ear ornament, presumed to be Javanese, Early Classic Period. Yale 2007.142.141 in Miksic 2011:169 Pl 46, dimensions: 2.08x2.02 cm 2.23 g. Courtesy Yale University Art Gallery.

Fig. 3.112 Richter 2000: 89, Connell private collection USA.

Fig. 3.113 Granulated ear ornaments, excavated at Oc Eo, Courtesy Oc Eo Cultural Sites Management.

19. EAR ORNAMENT

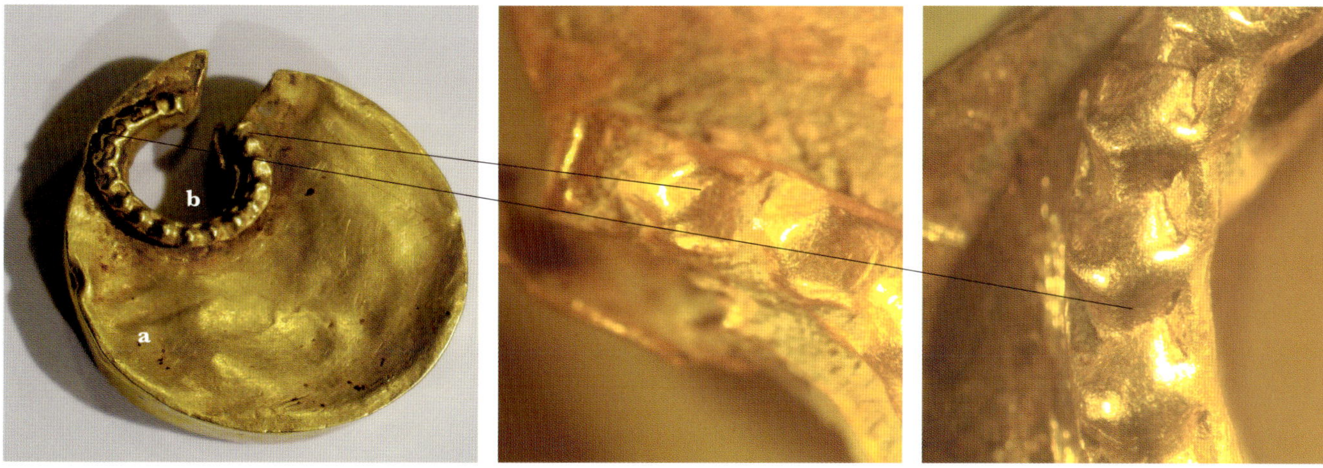

Figs. 3.114–3.116 The object is made of four pieces of hammered gold sheet with lengths of decorated gold wire soldered to the front and back. The decoration on the wire itself has been achieved by hammering and punching and the resulting tool marks are clearly visible.

Weight: 28.75 g
Width: 31.41 mm
Height: 33.92 mm
Elemental composition:
side a 89.14% gold, 9.45% silver, 1.17% copper, 0% tin,
side b 89.19% gold, 9.36% silver, 1.19% copper, 0% tin
Manufacture: hammered sheet with lengths of decorated gold wire soldered to the front and the back
Condition: complete
Evidence of use: some wear
Find location: the object was found by villagers just outside the east moat
Present location: Suriya Surapanich collection, U Thong

Figs. 3.117–3.118 The author examining the reverse of the ornament. Wear and burial patina still evident.

20. HAIR ORNAMENT WITH GREEN STONE AND BRAIDED ATTACHEMENT WITH GRANULATED DECORATION

Figs. 3.119–3.120 The attachment has become detached but there is no loss of material.

Weight: 8.91g
Weight of ornament and stone: 7.09 g
Weight of braided attachment: 1.82 g
Diameter: not determined
Height: not determined
Elemental composition:
ornament 90.18% gold, 7.27% silver, 0.5% copper, 0% tin,
attachment 91.09% gold, 7.29% silver, 1.04% copper, 0% tin,
Manufacture: the ornament is cast and the attachment mechanism is made of gold wires and granualtion on a backplate which was soldered onto the reverse
Condition: attachment has become detached
Evidence of use: none
Find location: corn field, U Thong district
Present location: Suriya Surapanich collection, U Thong

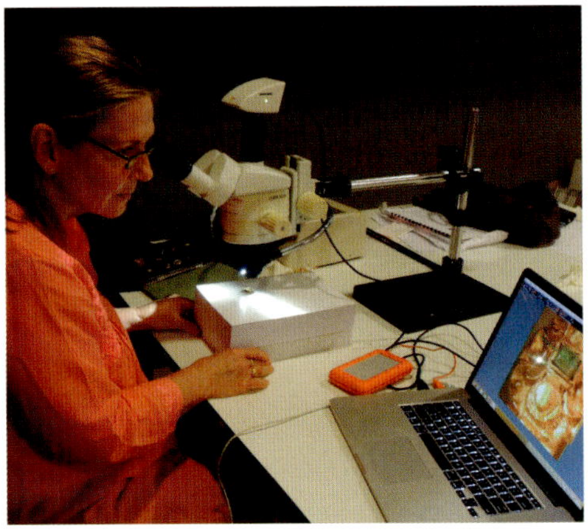

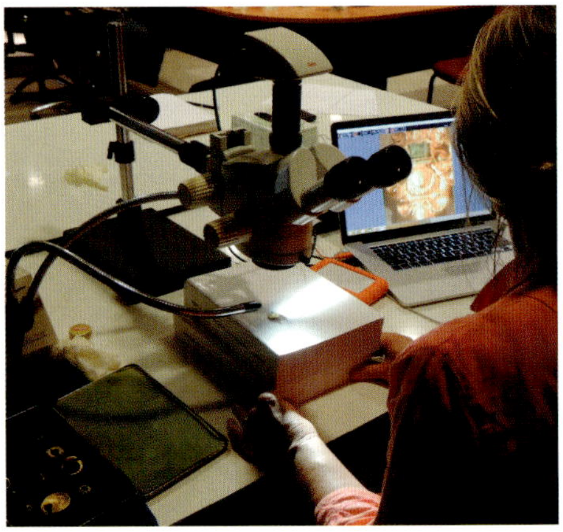

Figs. 3.121–3.122 The author examining the ornament under the microscope with a live digital image displayed on a connected computer screen.

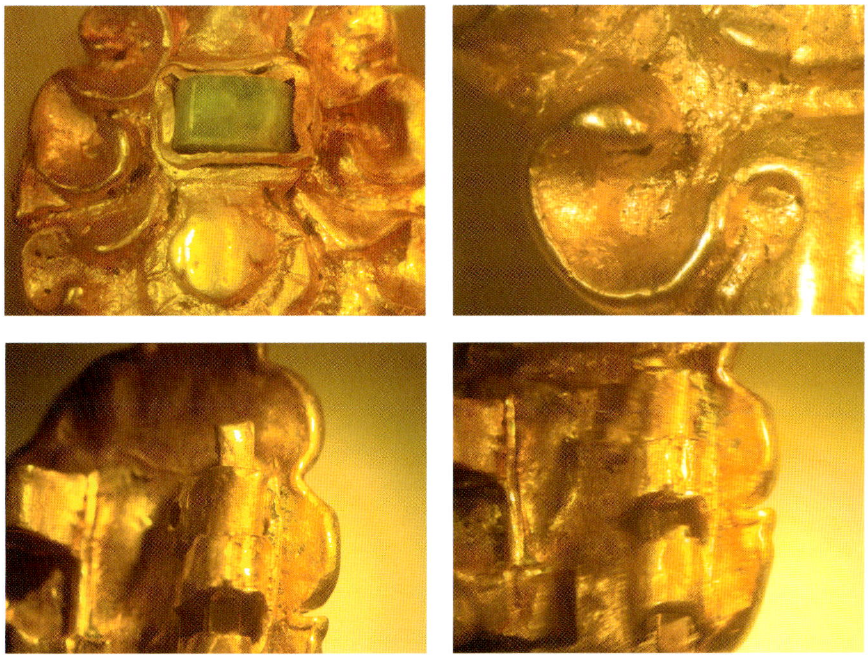

Fig. 3.12–3.126 The ornament is cast and the mount for the stone inlay is made separately, the appearance of the gold surface under the microscope confirms that all the decoration was achieved in the casting and there was no chasing of the detail after the casting. The attachment mechanism was soldered onto on a backplate which was in turn soldered to the reverse of the ornament.

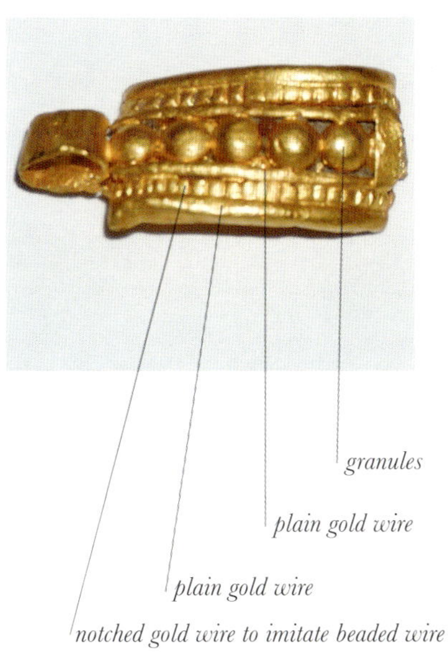

Fig. 3.127 The detached clasp is made of gold wires and granulation.

PARALLEL:

Fig. 3.128 Ornament found at Oc Eo (Miksic 2003 Pl 1.7).

21. EAR-CLASP WITH A DOUBLE CONE DROP AND GRANULATION

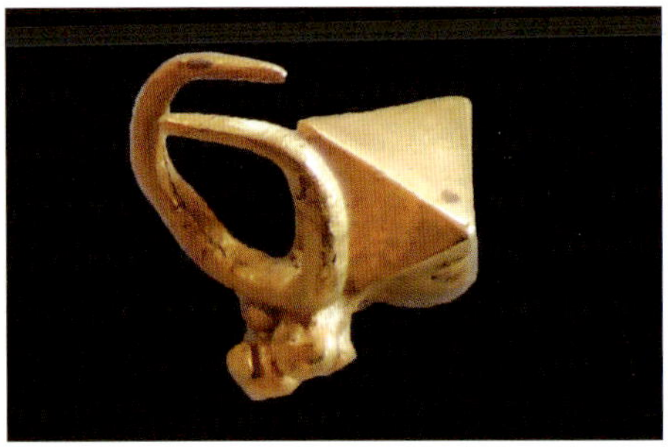

Fig. 3.129

Weight: 4.15 g
Width of bead: 7.01 mm
Manufacture: cast or hammered drop, hammered wire and granulation
Condition: complete
Evidence of use: no wear
Find location: field, U Thong district
Present location: Suriya Surapanich collection, U Thong

22. EAR-CLASP WITH A DOUBLE CONE DROP AND GRANULATION

Fig. 3.130 Another ear clasp similar but smaller than cat.no. 21.

Weight: 2.53 g
Width of bead: 5.45 mm
Manufacture: granulation and gold wire on hammered sheet
Condition: part of the attachment has broken off
Evidence of use: none
Find location: field, U Thong district
Present location: Suriya Surapanich collection, U Thong

PARALLEL:

Fig. 3.131 The ear ornament is similar to 2007.142.223 in Miksic 2011:163, Pl 42, early classical period

23. EAR CLASP IN THE FORM OF A BIRD

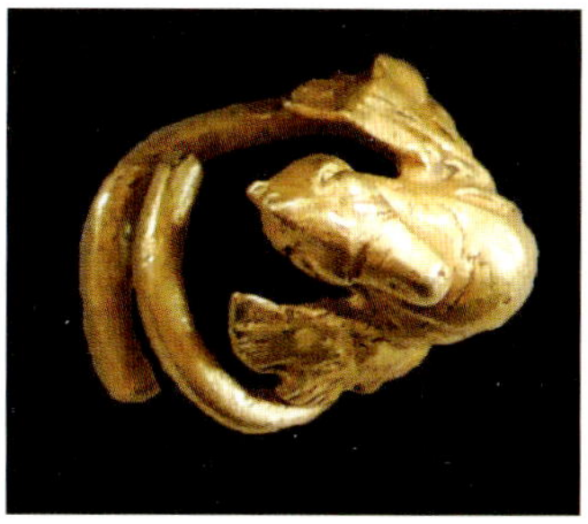
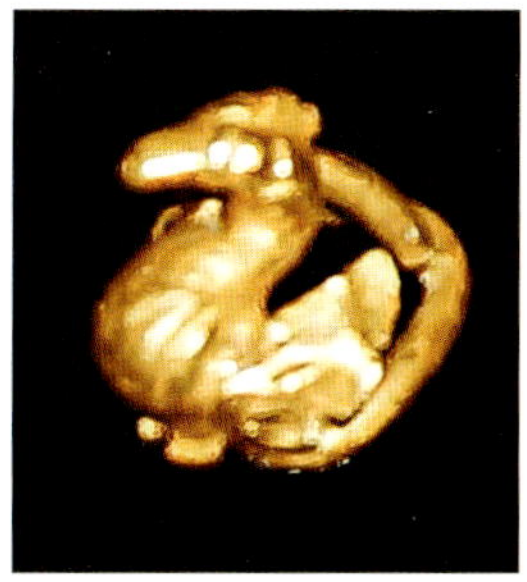

Weight: 2.31 g
Width: 8.37 mm
Height: 9.83 mm
Manufacture: cast bird with hammered wire
Condition: complete
Evidence of use: none
Find location: field, U Thong district
Present location: Suriya Surapanich collection, U Thong

Figs. 3.132–3.133

24. EAR CLASP IN THE FORM OF A VAJRA, INLAY NOW LOST

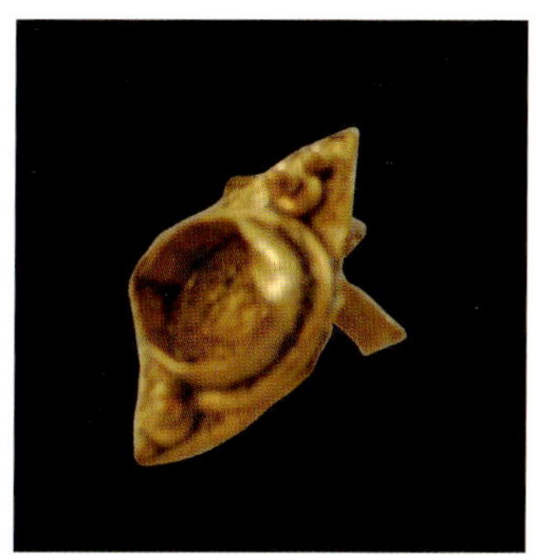

Figs. 3.134–3.135 Ear clasp in the form of a vajra, the god Indra's thunderbolt.

Weight: 0.3 g
Height: 10.38 mm
Width: 5.79 mm
Manufacture: hammered sheet with gold wire and granulation. Gold strip used for the attachment. Originally would have held an inlay
Condition: inlay now lost and part of the attachment has broken off
Evidence of use: unclear
Find location: field, U Thong district
Present location: Suriya Surapanich collection, U Thong

Fig. 3.136 Stone mould for producing decorated hammered gold sheet.

PARALLELS:

These small ear ornaments are sometimes described as bird rings used on the legs of pet birds. However, there is no evidence for this and it is perhaps more likely that they were fitted to the upper helix of the ear. Similar examples have been found at Oc Eo in Vietnam and sites in Java.

Fig. 3.137 Richter 2000 Pl 83. Private Collection USA.

25. ONAMENT MADE FROM A TUBE OF HAMMERED GOLD SHEET COVERED WITH COILED FLATTENED WIRE

Fig. 3.138 Objects such as these have been referred to as fused discs but examination under the microscope indicates that this example is made from a tube of hammered gold sheet covered with coiled flattened wire soldered into place.

Weight: not determined
Lenght: 11.32 mm
Diameter: 5.89 mm
Width: 0.98 mm
Manufacture: made from a tube of hammered sheet covered with coiled flattened wire soldered into place
A seam running the length of the tube is visible
Evidence of use: unclear
Find location: field, U Thong district
Present Location: Suriya Surapanich collection, U Thong

PARALLEL:

Fig. 3.139 Reinecke, Laychour & Sonetra 2009: 85 Pl 68. Ear ornament excavated at Prohear. The object is very heavy (16 g) (diam. 2 cm) and is probably solid cast rather than made of gold sheet wrapped in gold wire.

26. SPLIT RING MADE OF GRANULATION

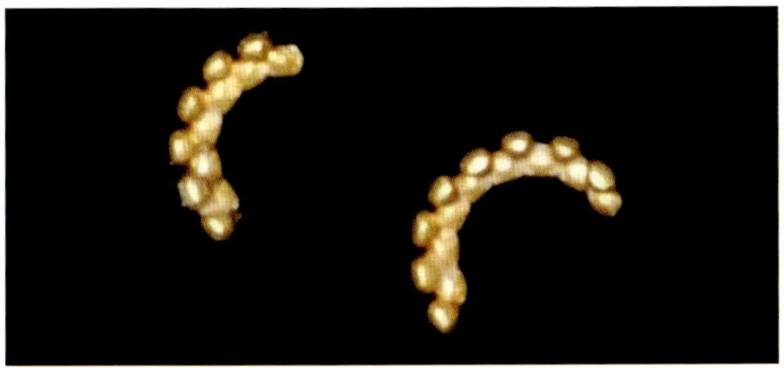

Fig. 3.140 The ring is entirely made up of gold granules fused together. There is no supporting wire or backplate.

Weight: 0.31 g
Width: 8.79 mm
Elemental composition: not determined
Manufacture: the ring is entirely made up of gold granules fused together. There is no supporting wire or backplate
Condition: broken in two, very fragile
Evidence of use: unclear
Find location: cornfield, U Thong district
Present location: Suriya Surapanich collection, U Thong

27. SPLIT EAR RING

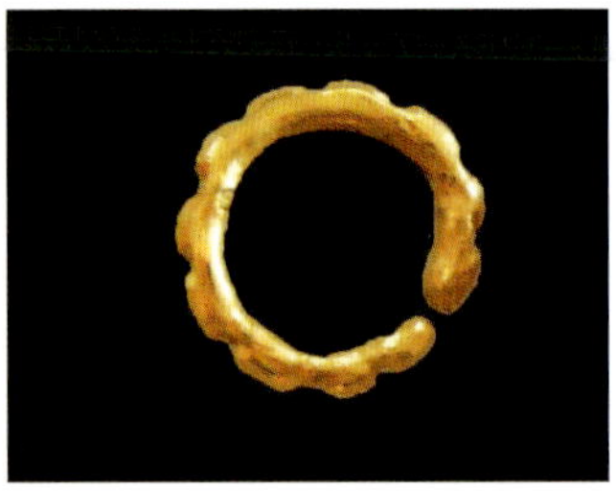

Fig. 3.141

Weight: 0.69 g
Width: 9.2 mm
Elemental composition: not determined
Manufacture: probably cast
Condition: good
Evidence of use: unclear
Find location: cornfield, U Thong district
Present location: Suriya Surapanich collection, U Thong

28. GOLD BEAD MADE IN GRANULATION

Fig. 3.142 The bead is made of gold granules fused onto a central wire.

Weight: 0.16 g
Width: 3.69 mm
Elemental composition: not determined
Manufacture: gold granules fused onto a central wire
Condition: complete
Evidence of use: unclear
Find location: cornfield, U Thong district
Present location: Suriya Surapanich collection, U Thong

29. LARGE MAN-SIZED FINGER RING WITH GREEN STONE

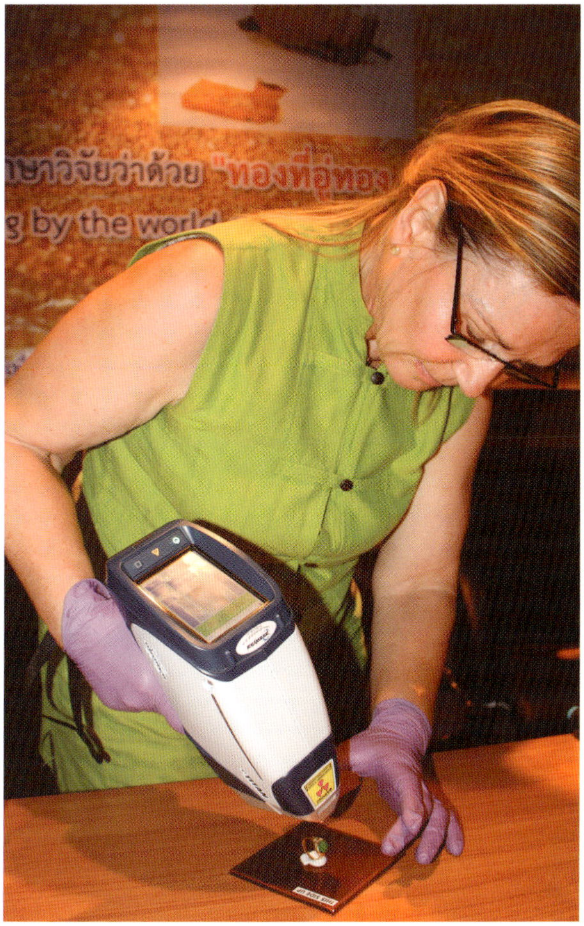

Weight: 14.88 g
Diameter: 27.19 mm
Height: 26.02 mm
Elemental composition: 90.18% gold, 7.27% silver, 0.5% copper, 0% tin.
Manufacture: the shank is cast and the mount is made seperately and soldered on. The green stone has not been identified.
Condition: good with original stone inlay
Evidence of use: the shank shows considerable wear
Find location: cornfield, U Thong district
Present location: Suriya Surapanich collection, U Thong

Fig 3.143 Author analysing the gold composition of the ring.

Fig 3.144 Reverse showing the gold mount soldered onto the cast shank. The shank shows considerable wear suggesting that the ring was in use over a prolonged period.

Fig 3.145 The ring still has its original stone in place. The stone has not been identified but may be a glass.

30. FINGER RING WITH STONE

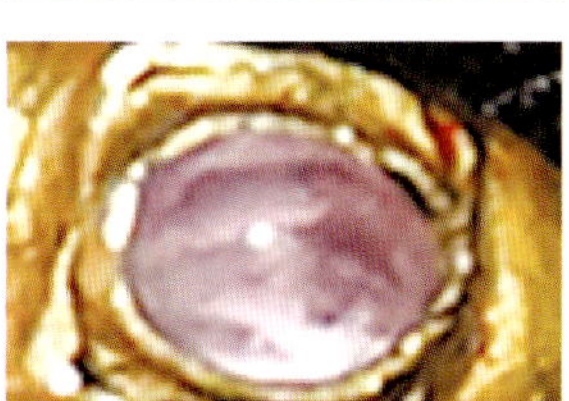

Weight: 2.82 g
Width: 18.06 mm
Height: 21.27 mm
Elemental composition: not determined
Manufacture: the shank is made of hammered sheet with a convex profile, the mount is made separately of hammered sheet and soldered onto the shank. The stone which appears to be original has not been identified.
Condition: much evidence of wear with original stone inlay
Evidence of use: the shank shows considerable wear
Find location: cornfield, U Thong district
Present location: Suriya Surapanich collection, U Thong

Figs. 3.146–3.147 The shank of the ring shows evidence of much wear, the original stone is still in place.

DVARAVATI GOLD OBJECTS FROM UTHONG IN THE BANGKOK NATIONAL MUSEUM

Figs. 3.148–3.150 Dvaravati gold objects from U Thong displayed in the gold case of the Bangkok National Museum.

The scientific equipment available to museum professionals today is small and compact and can be readily taken to exhibition spaces, thus precluding any risks in the transporting of objects and avoiding the additional costs of packing and transport. A stereomicroscope microscope and a hand held X-ray fluorescence analyzer were set up in the gold gallery of the Bangkok National Museum for a day in July 2015.

The objects were examined under the microscope in order to document their methods of manufacture and record evidence of use and repair. Digital images were simultaneously displayed on a connected computer screen which allowed the curators of the department to assess the objects during the examinations. The objects were weighed and their elemental composition was determined using surface X-ray fluorescence.

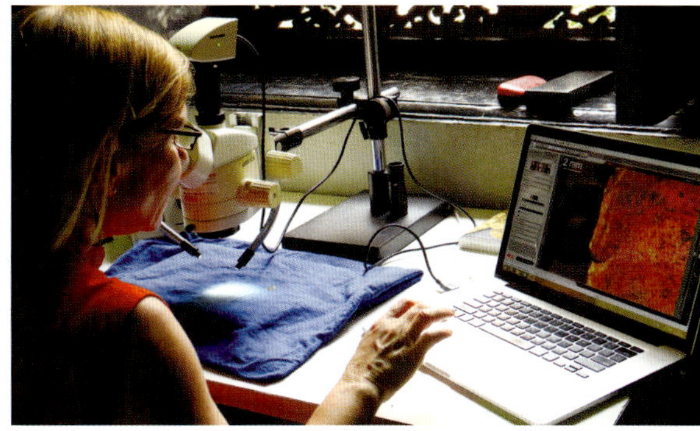

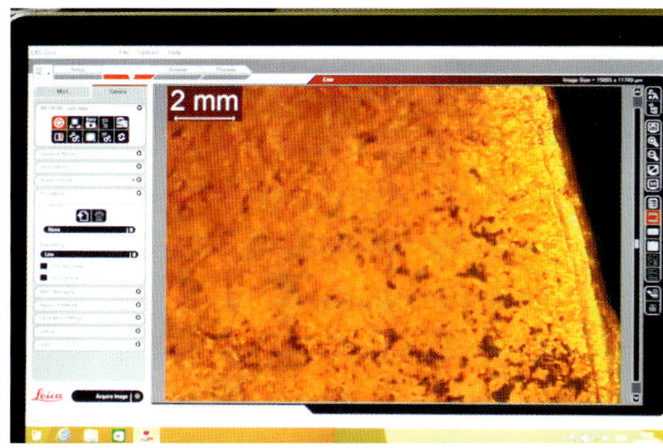

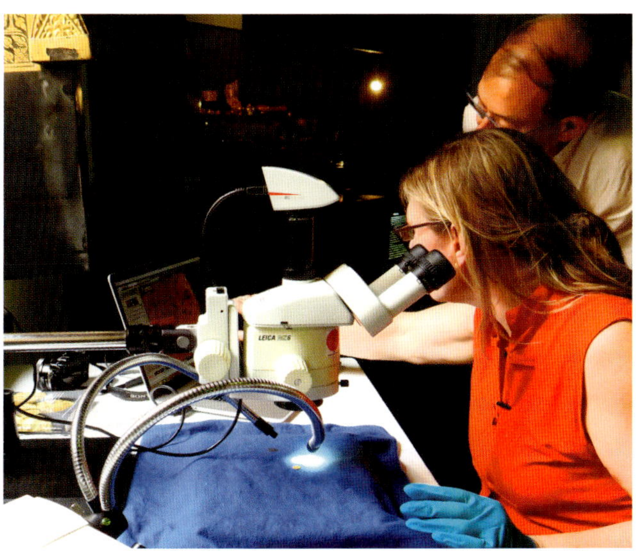

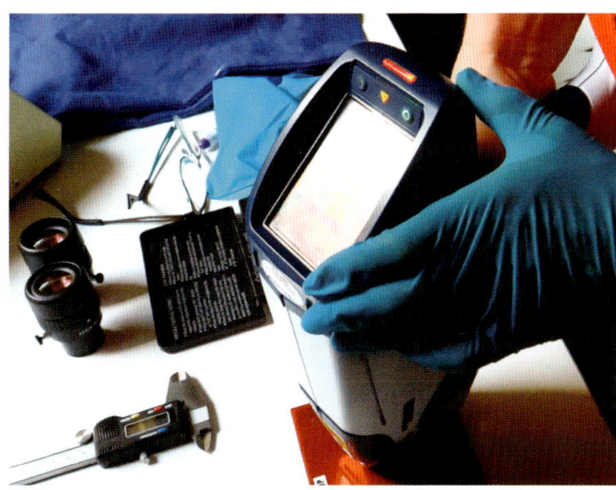

Figs. *3*.151–3.153 Digital images simultaneously displayed on a connected computer screen allowed assessment of the objects. *Figs. 3.154–3.155* The composition was determined using hand held X-ray fluorescence equipment and the weights of the items recorded.

31. GOLD PENDANT AND DECORATIVE BEAD NECKLACE

Fig. 3.156 The gold necklace is composed of 158 beads of at least nine different types with a central drop pendant. The beads include examples constructed from gold wire and individual granules, hammered gold sheet over clay cores of different shapes and cast beads.

Weight of pendant and beads: 29.25 g (including modern clasp)
Length of necklace as displayed: 300 mm (including beads and pendant)
Length of necklace as displayed beads only: 275 mm
Height of pendant excluding clasp: 22.07 mm
Height of pendant including clasp: 25.8 mm
Manufacture of pendant: cast with a small amount of reworking
Elemental analysis of pendant:
front: 94.26% gold, 4.77% silver, 0.29% copper
reverse: 93.05% gold, 5.39% silver and 0.5% copper
Manufacture of beads: nine types of bead were identified. These include beads constructed from gold wire and individual granules, hammered gold sheet over clay cores of different shapes and cast beads
Condition: complete
Evidence of use: evidence of wear over the surface
Find location: acquired in 1975 reportedly with many other gold items which formed part of a colonel's collection
Present location: National Museum Bangkok
Inventory number: not available

Fig. 3.157 The necklace is complete and shows evidence of wear.

POLYHEDRAL BEADS WITH GRANULATION

Made of wire and granulation in an openwork structure, these multi facetted wire beads have also been found at Khao Sam Kaeo in peninsula Thailand, at Pyu sites in Myanmar, at Oc Eo in Vietnam and at the Han site of Hepu in southern China (Pryce, Bellina and Bennett 2006; Bennett 2014; Demandt 2015 figs. 4 & 5). They are constructed using gold wire with individual gold granules, produced by melting small pieces of metal into spheres. During manufacture these spheres were held in place using a mixture of a powdered copper compound and an organic adhesive. When the assemblage is heated, the glue burns to carbon and the copper compound is reduced in situ to copper metal which diffuses into the surrounding gold. An almost invisible copper/gold alloy bond is formed directly at the point of contact between the granules and the gold wire.

Figs. 3.158–3.159 Polyhedral beads made of wire and granulation in an openwork structure. Diam: 5.56 mm.

Figs. 3.160–3.161 Polyhedral beads with an openwork structure. Diam: 7.8 mm.

One interesting feature of this type of bead is that they are not all made in the same manner. The author has examined chance finds in Myanmar which were clearly cast and still others on the art market which were made by soldering the granules in place. Until further study the author remains sceptical as to their authenticity.

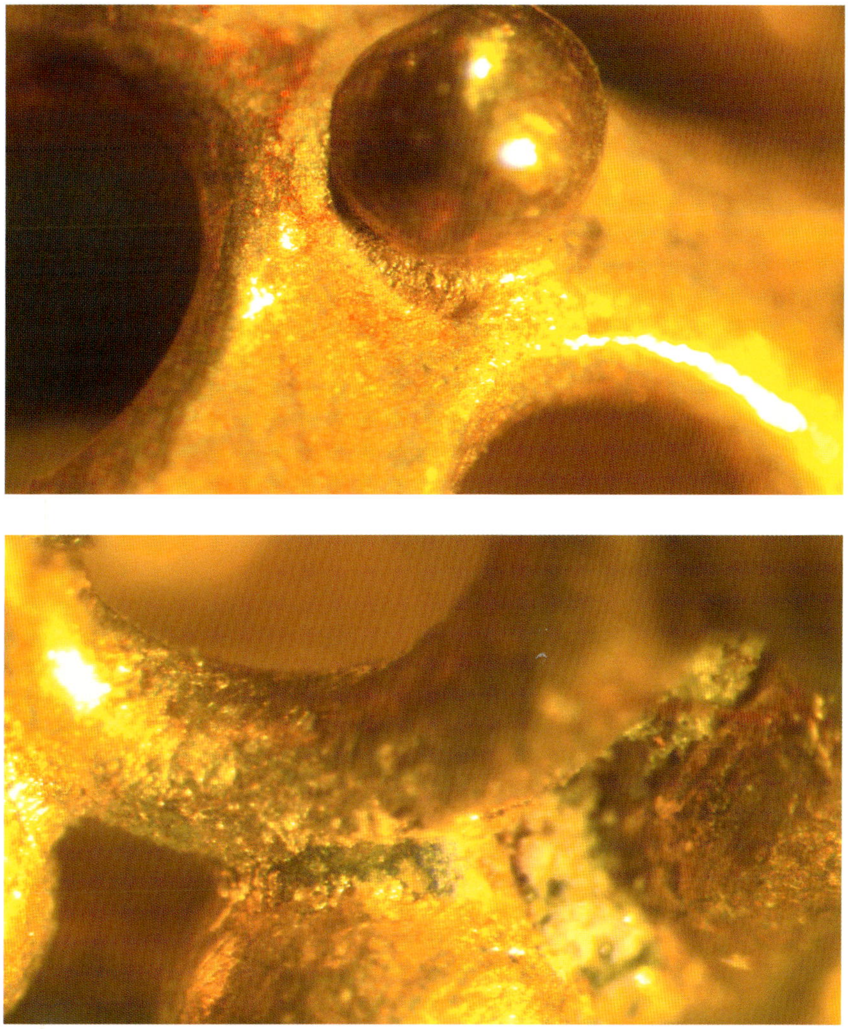

Figs. 3.162–3.163 The copper/gold alloy bond formed between the granules and the gold wire is almost invisible.

SQUARE BEADS WITH GRANULATION IN AN OPENWORK STRUCTURE

Figs. 3.164–3.165 Bead built up of gold wire and individual gold granules. Diam: 4.14 mm.

POLYHEDRAL BEADS WITH GRANUALTION AND INFILLED STRUCTURE

Fig 3.166 Wire and granulation applied to gold sheet. Diam: 6.43 mm.

GRANULATION BEAD

Figs. 3.167–3.168 Beads made entirely of individual gold granules fused together. Width: 3.17mm.

MELON BEADS

Fig. 3.169 Melon beads made of hammered sheet over a clay core.

ROUND-CONE SHAPED BEADS

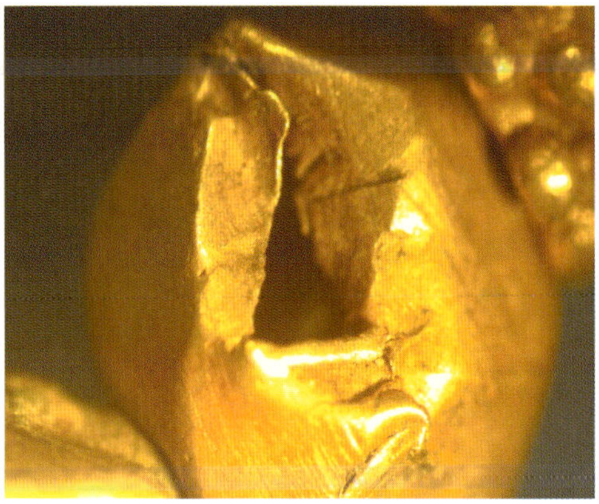

Width:	*4.82*	*mm*
Height:	*4.35*	*mm*

Figs. 3.170–3.171 Cone shaped bead and detail showing that these beads were made in two halves over a clay core.

OCTAGONAL BEADS

Width:	*4.35*	*mm*
Height:	*3.73*	*mm*

Fig. 3.172 Cast octagonal bead.

Figs. 3.173–3.174 Octagonal bead with cast surface.

CENTRAL DROP PENDANT IN THE SHAPE OF A FLOWER

Fig. 3.175

The central drop pendant in the form of a flower was cast with a small amount of hammering and chasing after casting. Two suspension holes were originally cast in at the time of manufacture but one broke and these were probably never used as the surviving hole shows no indication of any wear. The original holes were cast very close to the edge and the damage probably occurred at the time of or shortly after manufacture. Two additional replacement holes were made by simply piercing the gold and folding the excess metal over around the holes. The pendant was attached to the beaded necklace via these holes and interconnecting links. A gold pin was passed through one of the pierced holes on one side of the pendant, through a link of the necklace and then through the pierced hole on the other side.

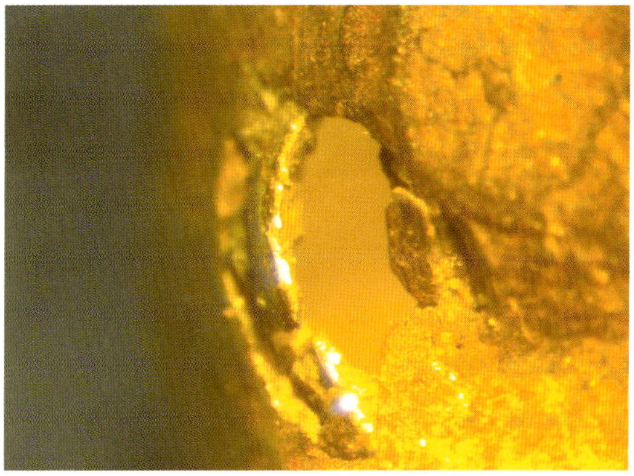

Figs. 3.176–3.177 Top of the pendant showing the original unbroken cast suspension hole.

Figs. 3.178–3.179 Top of the pendant showing the original cast suspension hole which broke. A second pierced suspension hole is visible at 90 degrees.

Fig. 3.180

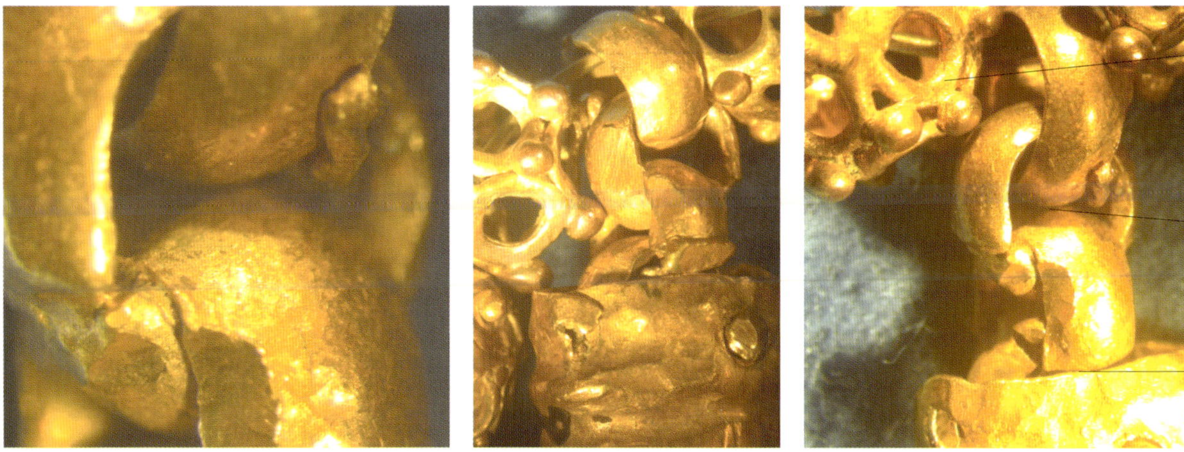

Figs. 3.181–3.183 The pendant was attached to the neckalce via interconnecting links.

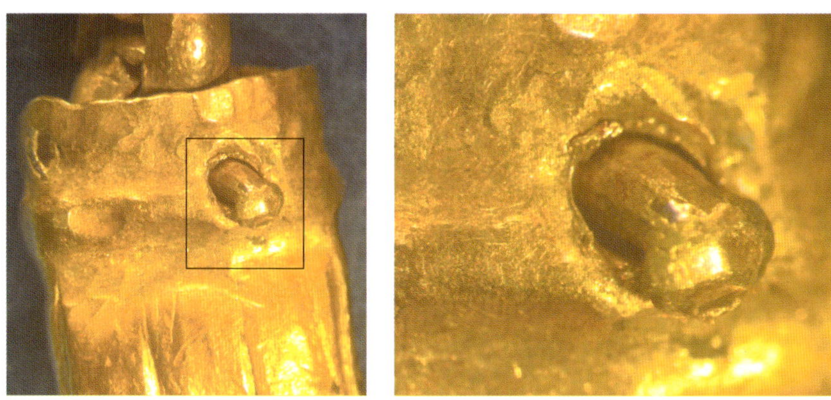

Figs. 3.184–3.185 Gold pin passed through the two pierced holes was used to secure the pendant to the links which in turn were attached to the beaded necklace.

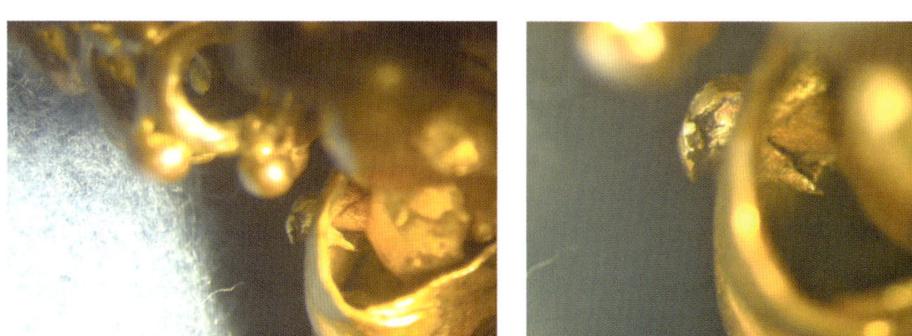

Figs. 3.186–3.187 The gold pin was passed through one of the pierced holes on one side of the pendant, through a gold link and then through the pierced hole on the other side.

Fig. 3.188

Gold composition
front: 94.26% gold, 4.77% silver and 0.29% copper
reverse: 93.05% gold, 5.39% silver and 0.5% copper

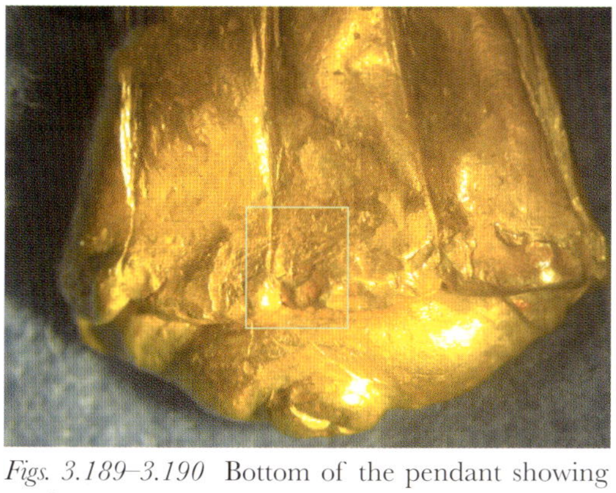

Figs. 3.189–3.190 Bottom of the pendant showing the cast surface with some hammering and chasing after casting.

32. GOLD PENDANT WITH GRANULATED DECORATION

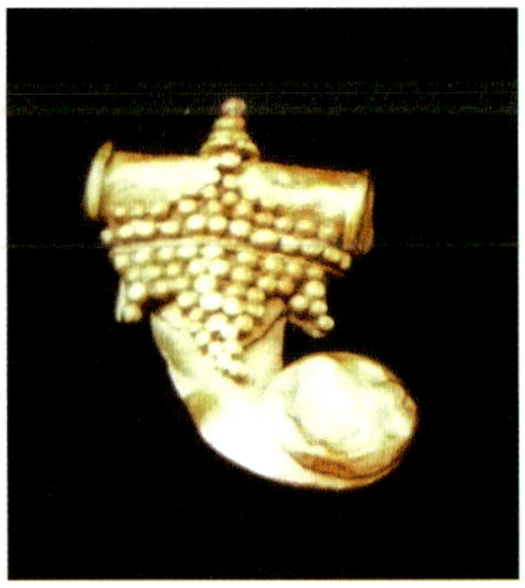

Figs. 3.191–3.192 The pendant is made up of pieces of gold sheet which are decorated with granulation and lengths of gold wire.

Weight of pendant: 3.17 g
Height: 20 mm
Width: 10 mm
Manufacture: made of pieces of gold sheet, decorated with granulation and lengths of wire
Elemental composition of pendant:
front: 94.26% gold, 4.77% silver, 0.29% copper, 0% tin
back: 93.05% gold, 5.39% silver, 0.5% copper, 0% tin
Area of granules front: 76.49% gold, 21.13% silver, 1.7% copper, 0.86% tin
Area of granules: 71.18% gold, 29.98% silver, 2.64% copper, 0.58% tin
Condition: complete and in very good condition
Evidence of use: evidence of wear over the surface
Find location: acquired in 1975 reportedly with many other gold items which formed part of a colonel's collection
Present location: National Museum Bangkok
Inventory number: not available

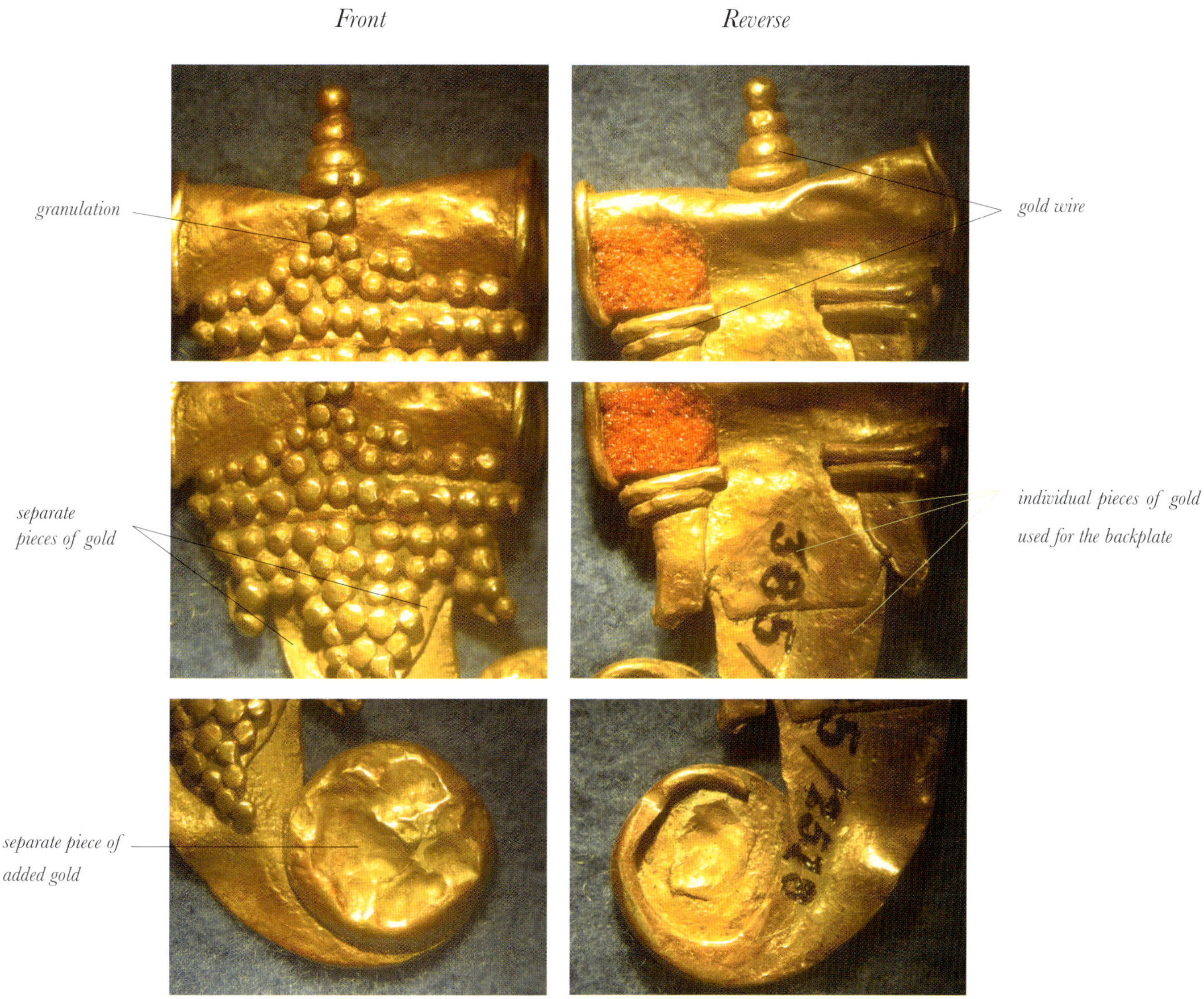

Figs. 3.193–3.198 The pendant was constructed using individual pieces of gold, lengths of gold wire and granualtion. The gold backplates were composed between 93.05%–94.26% gold, 4.77%–5.39% silver, 0.29%–0.5% copper. The area covered in granulation contained a higher copper content than that of the undecorated plain areas due to the copper salts used in the granulation process having diffused into the gold.

33. EAR ORNAMENT

Fig. 3.199 Ear ornament made of gold foil hammered over a clay core with ribbed decoration.

Fig. 3.200 The gold sheet was made in two halves and a join is visible around midsection.

Fig. 3.201 The expansion of the clay core has pushed the gold sheet covering off.

Height: 25 mm
Width: 30 mm
Manufacture: made of two pieces of gold foil hammered over a clay core with ribbed decoration
Condition: the clay core has expanded and there is some deformation to the gold sheet covering
Evidence of use: unclear
Find location: acquired in 1975 reportedly with many other gold items which formed part of a colonel's collection
Present location: National Museum Bangkok
Inventory number: not available

BIBLIOGRAPHY

Baptiste, Pierre, and Thierry Zéphir Eds. 2009. *Dvāvaratī: aux sources du Bouddhisme en Thaïlande*. Exhibition catalogue. Paris: Réunion des Musées Nationaux and Musée Guimet.

Barram, Andrew 2003. Dating 'Dvaravati'. *Bulletin of the Indo-Pacific Prehistory Association* 23: 59–62.

Barram, Andrew, and Ian Glover 2008. Re-thinking Dvāvaratī. In *Archaeology in Southeast Asia—from Homo erectus to the Living Traditions, Selected papers from the 11th International Conference of the European Association of Southeast Asian Archaeologists, Bougan, 25–29th September 2006,* Eds. J.P. Pautreau, P.S. Méry, V. Zeitoun & E. Rambault, Chiang Mai: Silkworm Press: 175–182.

Bellina, Bérénice 2001. Témoignages archéologiques d'échanges entre l'Inde et l'Asie du Sud-Est: Morphologie, morphométrie et techniques de fabrication des perles en agate et en cornaline. PhD diss., Université de la Sorbonne Nouvelle.

Bellina, Bérénice 2003. Beads, Social Change and Interaction between India and Southeast Asia. *Antiquity 77 (296)*: 285–97.

Bellina, Bérénice, and Ian Glover 2004. The Archaeology of Early Contact with India and the Mediterranean World, from the Fourth Century BC to the Fourth Century AD. In *Southeast Asia: From Prehistory to History* Eds. Ian Glover and Peter Bellwood, London: Routledge-Curzon: 68–88.

Bellina, Bérénice, and Praon Silapanth 2006. Khao Sam Kaeo and the Upper Thai Peninsula: Understanding the Mechnisms of Early Trans-Asiatic Trade and Cultural Exchange. In *Uncovering Southeast Asia's Past Selected papers from the 10th International Conference of the European Association of Southeast Asian Archaeologists, London 14–17th September 2004,* Eds. Bacus, E.A., Glover, I.C., and Piggott, V.C., Singapore: National University Press: 379–392.

Bellina, Bérénice 2007. Cultural Exchange between India and Southeast Asia: Production and Distribution of Hard Stone Ornaments (VI c. B. C. – VI c. A. D.). Maison des Sciences de l'Homme. Paris.

Bellina, Bérénice, Praon Silapanth, Boonyarit Chaisuwan Cholawit Thongcharoenchaikit, Jane Allan, Vincent Bernard, Brigitte Borell, Phaedra Bouvet, Cristina Castillo, Laure Dussubieux, Julie Malakie LaClair, Sachipan Srikanlaya, Sophie Peronnet, Oliver Pryce 2014. The Early Development of Coastal Polities in the Upper Thai-Malay in *Before Siam: Essays in Art and Archaeology*, Eds. Nicolas Revire and Stephen A. Murphy, River Books & The Siam Society, Bangkok: 69–89.

Bennett, Anna 1982. *The iron from Ban Don Ta Phet, Thailand.* Report (Unpublished). University of London: Institute of Archaeology.

Bennett, Anna 1988a. Copper Metallurgy in Central Thailand. PhD diss., Institute of Archaeology, University College London.

Bennett, Anna 1988b. Prehistoric Copper Smelting in Thailand in *Prehistoric Studies: the Stone Age and Metal Ages in Thailand*, Eds. Charoenwongsa, P. and Bronson, B., Thai Antiquity Working Group: 125–135, Bangkok.

Bennett, Anna 1989a. The contribution of metallurgical studies to South east Asian archaeology in *World Archaeology*, 20: 329–51.

Bennett, Anna 1989b. Sources of copper and tin ores in Prehistoric Thailand. Symposium Archaeometallurgie Von Kupfer und Eisen in West Europa, *Romisch Germanishe Zentralmuseum Mainz*: 526–532.

Bennett, Anna and Ian Glover 1992. Large Bronze Urns in Southeast Asia: Some New Finds and Reassessment. In *Southeast Asian Archaeology, 1990: Proceedings of the 3rd International Conference of the European Association of Southeast Asian Archaeologists*, Eds. Ian C. Glover. Centre for Southeast Asian Studies, University of Hull: 209–26.

Bennett, Anna 2010. Trading Gold in Early Asia. In *A Passage to Asia,* BOZAR, Centre for Fine Arts, Brussels: 63 –70.

Bennett, Anna 2013a. Protohistoric Iron Weapons and Tools from a Burial Site in West Central Thailand. In *The World of Iron* Eds. Humphries J, Rehren, Th., Archetype publication: 371–379.

Bennett, Anna 2013b. The Importance of Iron—its Development and Complexity in the Southeast Asian Iron Age. In *Selected Papers from the 12th International Conference of the European Association of Southeast-Asian Archaeologists, Leiden, September 2008.* IAS Publication series, Amsterdam University Press:107–121.

Bennett, Anna 2015a. Ancient Gold and Modern Fakes in Southeast Asia. In *Gold in Early Southeast Asia,* Eds. Barnes R, Stein E.N. and Diebold B. Selected papers from the symposium *Gold in Southeast Asia*, Yale University Art Gallery 13–14 May 2011. Monograph 64. New Haven: Yale Southeast Asia Studies: 183–236.

Bennett, Anna 2015b. Metallography, Experimental Smithing and Ethnographic Interpretation of Late Prehistoric Iron Billhooks from Mainland Southeast Asia. In Srinivasan S, Ranganathan S, Giumlia-Mair A (eds) Metals and Civilizations Proceedings of the Seventh International Conference on the Beginnings of the Use of Metals and Alloys (BUMA VII), Bangalore: National Institute of Advanced Studies: 68–77.

Bhumadhon, Phuthorn 2015. In *The Beads and Archaeology of U Thong*. Eds. Pongpanich, Bunchar and Bhumadhon, Phuthorn, Bangkok.

Boisselier, Jean 1965. Récentes Recherches Archéologiques en Thailande: Rapport Préliminaire de Mission (25 juillet–28 novembre 1964), *Arts Asiatiques 12*: 125–74.

Boisselier, Jean 1966. Ū-Thòng et son importance pour l'histoire de Thaïlande [et] Nouvelles données sur l'histoire ancienne de Thaïlande, *Bōrānwitthayā rīrang Muang Ū Thong*, Bangkok, Krom Sinlapakon, 2509 [1966]: 161–176.

Boisselier, Jean 1968. Nouvelles connaissances archaeologiques de la ville d'Uthong. Bangkok.

Borell, Brigitte 2008a. The Early Byzantine Lamp from Pong Tuk. *The Journal of the Siam Society 96*, Bangkok: 1–26.

Borell, Brigitte 2008b. Some Western Imports Assigned to the Oc Eo Period Reconsidered. In *Archaeology in Southeast Asia—from Homo erectus to the Living Traditions, Selected papers from the 11th International Conference of the European Association of Southeast Asian Archaeologists, Bougan, 25–29th September 2006*, Eds. J.P. Pautreau, P.S. Méry, V. Zeitoun & E. Rambault, Chiang Mai: Silkworm Press: 167–174.

Borell, Brigitte 2014. The Power of Images – Coin Portraits of Roman Emperors on Jewellery Pendants in Early Southeast Asia in *Zeitschrift für archäologie aussereurpäischer kulturen*, 6. Reichert Verlag, Wiesbaden: 7–43.

Borell, Brigitte (forthcoming) Roman Coins and Derivatives. Pendants Imitating the Design of a Roman Coin from Sites in Southeast Asia. Paper presented at the 14th International Conference of the European Association of Southeast Asian Archaeologists, Dublin, September 2012.

Borell, Brigitte, Bérénice Bellina, Boonyarit Chaisuwan 2014. Contacts between the Upper Thai-Malay Peninsula and the Mediterranean World, in *Before Siam: Essays in Art and Archaeology*, Eds. Nicolas Revire and Stephen A. Murphy. Bangkok: River Books & The Siam Society: 98–117.

Bronson, Bennet 1986. Glass and Beads at Khuan Lukpad. In *Southeast Asian Archaeology, 1986: Proceedings of the First Conference of the Association of Southeast Asian Archaeologists in Western Europe, Institute of Archaeology, University College London, 8–10th September 1986*, Eds. Ian Glover and Emily Glover Oxford: British Archaeological Series [BAR] 561:139–83.

Brown, Robert 1996. *The Dvaravati Wheels of the Law and the Indianization of South East Asia*. Studies in Asian Art and Archaeology, Vol. 18, Ed. Fontein, Jan, Leiden and New York: E. J. Brill.

Brown, Robert 2014. Dvaravati Sculpture. In *Lost Kingdoms: Hindu Buddhist Sculpture of Early Southeast Asia*, The Metropolitan Museum of Art, Yale University Press: 189–191.

Bunker, Emma 2008. Amalgam Gilding in Khmer Culture. In *Interpreting Southeast Asia's Past: Monument, Image, and Text* Eds. Elisabeth A. Bacus, Ian C. Glover, and Peter Sharrock European Association of Southeast Asian Archaeologists, Singapore: National University of Singapore Press: 296–305.

Christie, Jan Wisseman 2015. Gold and Early Javanese Inscriptions. In *Gold in Early Southeast Asia*, Barnes R, Stein E.N. Diebold B, selected papers from the symposium *Gold in Southeast Asia*. Yale University Art Gallery 13–14 May 2011: 75–88.

Coedès, George 1928. Les Collections Archéologiques du Musée National de Bangkok *Ars Asiatica* 12. Paris: G. Van Oest.

Datta, P.K, P.K. Chattopadhyay, and A. Ray 2007. New Evidence for High-Tin Bronze in Ancient Bengal, *Society of Archaeological Scineces Bulletin*, 30 (2): 13–16.

Dermandt, Michele 2015. Early Gold Ornaments of Southeast Asia: production, trade and consumption. *Asian Perspectives*, 54 (2): 305 – 330.

Dube, R.K., 2003. Suvarnabhumi, and Suvarnadvipa; origin, identity, and its richness in gold in ancient and medieval Times. *Bulletin of the Metals Museum* 36: 3–23.

Fabris, G. and F.E. Treloar 1980. X-Ray Fluorescence and Atomic Absorption Analysis of Sarawak Gold Artefacts, *Archaeometry* 22 (1): 93–98.

Fine Arts Department 2002. Archaeology of Kok-Chang Din (in Thai), Bangkok: Fine Arts Department.

Gallon, Mathew 2014. Monuments and Identity at the Dvaravati Town of Kamphaeng Saen, in *Before Siam: Essays in Art and Archaeology*, edited by Nicolas Revire and Stephen A. Murphy. Bangkok: River Books & The Siam Society: 331–351.

Glover, Ian, Pisit Charoenwongsa, Bryan Alvey and Nawarat Kammounket 1984. The Cemetery of Ban Don Ta Phet, Thailand: Results from the 1980–81 Excavation Season in *South Asian Archeology, 1981:Proceedings of the Sixth International Conference of the Association of South Asian Archeologists in Western Europe, Held in Cambridge University, 5–10 July 1981*, edited by Bridget Allcin, pp. 319 –30. Cambridge: Cambridge University Press.

Glover, Ian 1990a. Ban Don Ta Phet: the 1984–85 Excavation. In *Southeast Asian Archaeology, 1986: Proceedings of the First Conference of the Association of Southeast Asian Archaeologists in Western Europe, Institute of Archaeology, University College London, 8–10th September 1986*, Eds. Ian Glover and Emily Glover. Oxford: British Archaeological Series [BAR] 561:139–83.

Glover, Ian 1990b. *Early Trade between India and Southeast Asia: A Link in the Development of a World Trading system.* Occasional Paper No 16, University of Hull: Centre for South-East Asian Studies. 2nd revised edition.

Glover, Ian 1996a. The Southern Silk Road: Archaeological Evidence for Early Trade between India and Southeast Asia, In *Ancient Trades and Cultural Contacts in Southeast Asia*, Bangkok: The Office of the National Culture Commission: 57–95.

Glover, Ian 1996b. The Archeological Evidence for Early Trade between India and Southeast Asia. In *The Indian Ocean in Antiquity*. London: Kegan Paul International: 365 –400.

Glover, Ian 2010a. The Dvaravati Gap—Linking Prehistory and History in Early Thailand. *Bulletin of the Indo-Pacific Prehistory Association*, 30: 79–86.

Glover, Ian 2010b. Thinking about Dvaravati. In *Abhinandanamālā: Nandana Chutiwongs Felicitation Volume,* Eds. Leelananda Prematilleke et al., Bangkok: SPAFA Regional Centre of Archeology and Fine Arts, in collaboration with the Abhinandanamālā Committee, Colombo: 47–65.

Glover, Ian and Bellina Bérénice 2011. Ban Don Ta Phet and Khao Sam Kaeo: The Earliest Indian Contacts Re-assessed. In *Early Interactions between South and Southeast Asia: Reflections on Cross-Cultural Exchange,* Eds. Pierre-Yves Manguin, A. Mani, and Geoff Wade, Nalanda-Sriwijaya Series 2. Singapore: Institute of Southeast Asian Studies, New Delhi: Manohar India: 17–45.

Glover, Ian and Anna Bennett 2012. The High-Tin Bronzes of Thailand. In *Scientific Research on Ancient Asian Metallurgy: Proceedings of the Fifth Forbes Symposium at the Freer Gallery of Art,* Eds. Paul Jett, Blythe McCarthy and Janet G. Douglas, London, Archetype Publications: 101–14.

Glover, Ian and Shahnaj Husne Jahan 2014. An Early Northwest Indian-Decorated Bronze Bowl From Khao Sam Kaeo, in *Before Siam, Essays in Art and Archaeology,* Eds. Nicolas Revire and Stephen Murphy, Bangkok. River Books & The Siam Society: 9–14.

Glover, Ian 2015. Ancient Collectors and archaeologists with special reference to Southeast Asia. In *Gold in Early Southeast Asia,* Eds. Barnes R, Stein E.N. Diebold B, selected papers from the symposium *Gold in Southeast Asia*. Yale University Art Gallery 13–14th May 2011: 237–251.

Guy, John 2014. *Lost Kingdoms: Hindu Buddhist Sculpture of Early Southeast Asia,* The Metropolitan Museum of Art, Yale University Press.

Higham, Charles 2001. *The Civilization of Angkor*. Berkeley and Los Angeles: University of California Press.

Higham, Charles 2014. *Early Mainland Southeast Asia From First Humans to Angkor.* River Books, Bangkok.

Hudson, Bob 2003. Dental Wealth. *Archaeology* 56 (4):10.

Hung, Hsiao-Chun, Yoshiyuki Iizuka and Peter Bellwood, 2006. Taiwan Jade in the Context of Southeast Asian Archaeology. In *Uncovering Southeast Asia's Past. Selected papers from the 10th International Conference of the European Association of Southeast Asian Archaeologists, London 14–17th September 2004,* Eds. Bacus, E.A., Glover, I.C., and Piggott, V.C., Singapore. National University Press: 203–215.

Hung, Hsiao-Chun and Peter Bellwood 2010. Movement of Raw Materials and Manufactured Goods across the South China Sea after 500 BCE: From Tawain to Thailand and Back. In *50 years of Archaeology in Southeast Asia: Essays in Honour of Ian Glover*, Eds. Bellina, Berenice, Bacus Elisabeth, Pryce Oliver, and Christie, Jan Wisseman. Bangkok, River Books: 235–245.

Indrawooth, Phasook 1999. *Dvāravatī—a critical study based on archaeological evidence,* Bangkok: Silpakorn (in Thai with English summary).

Indrawooth, Phasook 2004. The Archaeology of the Early Buddhist Kingdoms of Thailand. In *Southeast Asia from Prehistory to History*, Eds. Glover, Ian and Bellwood, P. London Routledge/Curzon: 120–148.

Indrawooth, Phasook 2008. Recent research on Dvaravati cultural workshop sites in Petchaburi province, Central Thailand. In *Interpreting Southeast Asia's Past: Monument, Image, and Text,* Eds. Elisabeth A. Bacus, Ian C. Glover, and Peter Sharrock, European Association of Southeast Asian Archaeologists 10, Singapore: National University of Singapore Press: 306–322.

Indrawooth, Phasook 2009. Un antique royaume urbanisé de Thaïlande. In Baptiste, Pierre and Zéphir, Thierry (eds.) *Dvāravatī: aux sources du bouddhisme en Thaïlande,* Paris. Réunion des muses nationaux: 31–45.

Kangle, R.P. 1960. The *Kautiliya Arthasastra.* Part 2: *An English Translation with Critical and Explanatory Notes*. Bombay: University of Bombay Press.

Lê Thị Liên 2006. *Nghê thuâ Phât giáo & Hindu giáo (Buddhist and Hindu art in the Cuu Long River Delta prior to the 10th century AD)* Hanoi: Thégiôi.

Lê Thi Lien 2011. Hindu Deities in Southern Vietnam: Images on Small Archaeological Artefacts in *Early Interactions Between South and Southeast Asia: Reflections on Cross-cultural Exchange,* Eds. Pierre-Yves Manguin, A. Mani and Geoff Wade, Nalanda-Sriwijaya Series 2. Singapore: Institute of Southeast Asian Studies; New Delhi, Manohar India: 407–31.

Lê Thi Lien 2013. Brahmi Inscription from Archaeological Sites in Southern Vietnam during the 1st Millenium CE. In *Advancing Southeast Asian Archaeology 2103*, selected papers from the first SEAMEO SPAFA International Conference, Chonburi, Thailand.

Lê Thị Liên and Michael Witzel 2013. Bàn về văn khắc Brahmi và tiểu tượng Hindu giáo thể hiện trên các mảnh vàng phát hiện ở Cát Tiên, Lâm Đồng [Discussion on Brahmi inscriptions and Hindu iconography presented on the gold plaques found from Cat Tien, Lam Dong], in *Vietnam Review of Indian and Asian Studies*, Institute of Indian and Southwest Asian Studies, 12 (13): 27–36.

Lê Thị Liên 2014. Hindu-Buddhist sculpture in Southern Vietnam: Evolution of Icons and Styles to the eighth century in *Lost Kingdoms: Hindu Buddhist Sculpture of Early Southeast Asia*. The Metropolitan Museum of Art, Yale University Press: 118–12.

Lertrit, S. 2001. Ceramic Chronology for Central Thailand: A View from the Pa Sak River Valley. PhD dissertation, Department of Anthropology, Washington State University.

Loofs, Helmut 1970. A brief account of the Thai-British Archaeological Expedition 1965–1970. *Archaeology and Physical Anthropology in Oceania* V (3): 177–84.

Loofs, Helmut 1979. Problems of Continuity between the pre-Buddhist and Buddhist Periods in Central Thailand, with special reference to U Thong In *Early South East Asia* Eds. R.B.Smith and W.Watson. Oxford University Press: 342–351.

Majumdar, Ramesh Chandra [1936] 1986. *Suvarṇadvīpa: Ancient Indian Colonization in the Far East,* New Delhi: Gian.

Majumdar, R.C.1953. Inscriptions of Kambuja. Calcutta: Asiatic Society.

Malleret, L. 1962. *L'archéologie du Delta du Mékong.* Vol.3 of *La culture du Fou-Nan.* Publications de l'École Française d'Extrême-Orient 43. Paris: École Française d'Extrême-Orient.

Manguin, P.Y. 2004. The Archaeology of Early Maritime polities of Southeast Asia in *Southeast Asia: From Prehistory to History* Eds. Ian Glover and Peter Bellwood, London: Routledge-Curzon: 282–313.

Manning, A., E. E. McKinnon and F. E. Treloar 1980. Analysis of Gold Artefacts from Kota Cina Site Near Medan, Sumatra. *Journal of the Malaysian Branch of the Royal Asiatic Society*.

Meltzer, Gudrun and Lore Sander 2006. A Copper Scroll Inscription from the Time of the Alchon Huns. In *Buddhist Manuscripts in the Schøyen Collection,* Eds. Jens Braarvig et al., vol. 3. Oslo: Hermes Publishing: 251–78.

Miksic, John 1990. *Old Javanese Gold*. Singapore, Ideation.

Miksic, John 2003. The Beginning of Trade in Ancient Southeast Asia: The Role of Oc Eo and Lower Mekong River. In *Art and Archaeology of Fu Nan: pre-Khmer Kingdom of the lower Mekong Valley*, Ed. J. C. M. Khoo:1–34. Bangkok: Orchid Press.

Miksic, John 2011. *Old Javanese Gold: The Hunter Thompson Collection at Yale University Art Gallery.* New Haven, CT: Yale University Press.

Moore, Elisabeth 2007. *Early Landscape of Myanmar*: River Books, Bangkok.

Natapintu, Surapol 1988. Current Research on Ancient Copper-Base Metallurgy in Thailand. In *Prehistoric Studies: the Stone Age and Metal Ages in Thailand,* Eds. Charoenwongsa, P. and Bronson, B. Bangkok: Thai Antiquity Working Group: 107–24.

Ogden, Jack 2004. Connections between Islam, Europe, and the Far East in the Medieval Period: Evidence of Jewellery Technology in *Scientific Research in the Field of Asian Art: Proceedings of the First Forbes Symposium at the Freer Gallery of Art Symposium*. London, Archetype Publications: 2–7.

Pigott, Vince 1982. The Innovation of Iron: Cultural Dynamics in Technological Change. *Expedition* 25 (1): 20 –25.

Pigott, Vince, Andrew Weiss, and Surapol Natapintu 1997. Archaeology of Copper Production: Excavations in the Khao Wong Prachan Valley, Central Thailand in *Proceedings of the Fourth International Conference of the European Asssociation of South-east Asian Archaeologists.* Rome, 28th September–4th October 1992, Eds. R. Ciarla and F. Rispoli. Istituto Italiano per l'Africa e l'Oriente: 119–157.

Pigott, Vince, and Roberto Ciarla 2007. On the Origins of Metallurgy in Prehistoric Southeast Asia: The view from Thailand. In *Metals and mines: Studies in Archeometellarurgy,* Eds. S. La Niece, D. Hook, and P. Craddock. London: Archetype Publications in association with the British Museum: 76–88.

Pigott, Vince 2012. Looking East: The Coming of Tin Bronze in the Context of Bronze Age Trans-Eurasian Exchange—An Overview. In *Scientific Research on Ancient Asian Metallurgy. Proceedings of the Fifth Forbes Symposium at the Freer Gallery of Art,* Archetype Publications in association with the Freer Gallery of Art, Smithsonian Institution.

Pongpanich, Bunchar 2009. *Beyond Beads,* Bangkok: Matichon Publishing House.

Pongpanich, Bunchar and Phuthorn Bhumadhon 2015. *The Beads of and Archaeology of U Thong*. In Thai, Bangkok.

Pryce, Oliver, Bellina Bérénice and Anna Bennett 2008. The Development of Metal Technologies in the Upper Thai-Malay Penininsula: Initial Interpretation of the Archaeometallurgical Evidence from Khao Sam Kaeo. *BEFEO* 93:295–315.

Quaritch Wales, Horace Geoffrey 1937. *Towards Angkor in the Footsteps of the Indian Invader,* London, Harrap.

Quaritch Wales, Horace Geoffrey 1969. *Dvāravatī. The Earliest Kingdom of Siam (6th–11th century A.D.).* London, Bernard Quaritch Ltd.

Ray, Himanshu Prabha 1994. *Winds of Change: Buddhism and the Maritime Links of Early South Asia*. New Delhi, Oxford University Press.

Ray, Himanshu Prabha 2014. Multi-religious Linkage across the Bay of Bengal during the First Millenuium CE in *Before Siam: Essays in Art and Archaeology*, Eds. Nicolas Revire and Stephen A. Murphy. Bangkok, River Books & The Siam Society: 134–151.

Reinecke, Andreas 2012. Prohear, an Iron Age Burial site on Southeastern Cambodia: Preliminary Report after Three Excavavations. In *Crossing Borders in Southeast Asian Archaeology,* Eds. Mai Lin Tjoa-Bonatz, Andreas Reinecke, and Dominik Bonatz. European Association of Southeast Asian Archaeologists. Singapore, National University of Singapore Press: 268–84.

Reinecke, Andreas 2015. Ancient Gold and Silver Jewellery and the Beginnings of Gold Working in Mainland Southeast Asia in *Gold in Early Southeast Asia,* Eds.Barnes R, Stein E.N. and Diebold B, selected papers from the symposium *Gold in Southeast Asia*. Yale University Art Gallery 13–14 May 2011. Monograph 64. New Haven: Yale Southeast Asia Studies: 125–166.

Reinecke, Andreas and Nguyen Thi Thanh Luyen 2009. Recent Discoveries in Vietnam: Gold Masks and Other Precious Items. *Arts of Asia* 39 (5): 58–67.

Reinecke, Andreas, Vin Laychour, Seng Soneta 2009. *The first Golden Age of Cambodia: Excavation at Prohear.* Bonn, German Foreign Office.

Richter, Anne 2000. *The Jewelry of Southeast Asia*. London: Thames and Hudson.

Riederer, Josef 1994. The Goldsmith's Techniques: The Technological Analysis of Early Gold Objects from Java. In *Old Javanese Gold (4–15th Century): An Archaeometrical Approach*, Ed. W. H. Kal. Amsterdam KIT: 46–57.

Schlosser, Sandra, Andreas Reinecke, Roland Schwab, Ernst Pernicka, Seng Sonetra and Vin Laychour 2012. Early Cambodian Gold and Silver from Prohear: Composition, Trace Elements and Gilding. *Journal of Archaeogical Science* 39: 2877–87.

San Thaiyanonda 2011. Cultural development of ancient communities at Mueang U Thong, PhD diss., Silpakorn University, Bangkok.

Scott, David 2013. Modern Antiquities: The Looted and the Faked. *International Journal of Cultural Property* 20:49–75.

Skilling, Peter 1999. A Buddhist inscription form Go Xoai, Southern Vietnam and Notes towards the classification of Ye Dharma Inscriptions in 80 pi satsadachan Dr Prasert Na Nakhon: Ruam botkhwam wichakan dan charuk lae ekasanboram (80 years: A collection of articles on epigraphy and ancient documents published on the occasion of the celebration of the 80th birthday of Prof. Dr. Prasert Na Nagara). Bangkok, Borisat Phikhanet Printing Center Chamkat: 171–87.

Skilling, Peter 2003. *Dvāvarati:* Recent Revelations and Research, In *Dedications to Her Royal Highness Princess Galyani Vadhana Krom Luang Naradhiwas Rajanagarindra on her 80th birthday.* Ed. Chris Baker. Bangkok, Siam Society: 87–112.

Skilling, Peter 2009. L'enigma de Si Thep In *Dvāvaratī: aux sources du Bouddhisme en Thaïlande*, Eds. Baptiste, Pierre and Thierry, Zéphir. Exh. cat. Paris: Réunion des Musées Nationaux and Musée Guimet: 107–113.

Skilling, Peter 2011. Buddhism and the Circulation of Ritual in Early Peninsular Southeast Asia, In *Early Interactions between South and Southeast Asia: Reflections on Cross-Cultural Exchange,* Eds. Pierre-Yves Manguin, A. Mani, and Geoff Wade, Nalanda-Sriwijaya Series 2. Singapore: Institute of Southeast Asian Studies. New Delhi: Manohar India: 371–84.

Skilling, Peter 2015. The Circulation of Artefacts Engraved with 'Apramāda' and Other Mottos in Southeast Asia and India: A Preliminary Report. In *Annual Report of The International Research Institute for Advanced Buddhology at Soka University for the Academic Year 2014,* V(XVIII). Soka University, Tokyo: 63–77.

Stambolov, T., 1999. Gold Mines, Ancient Indonesian Ornaments, and the Exact Sciences in *Precious Metals in Early South East Asia*, Rd. W. H. Kal. Amsterdam, KIT: 23–26.

Srisuchat, Amara 1996. Merchants and Markets: Archaeological Evidence in Thailand Concerning Maritime Trade Interaction between Thailand and Other Countries before the 16th Century AD. In *Ancient Trades and Cultural Contacts in Southeast Asia,* Bangkok, Office of the National Cultural Commission: 237–266.

Supamas Doungsakun 2005. Palaeo-environmental study at Khok Chang Din Ruins, U Thong district, Suphanburi province M.Sc diss., Mahidol University, Bangkok.

Swan, Rachel and David Scott 1990. Gold Work from Kota Cina: A Technical Study. In *Southeast Asian Archaeology, 1986: Proceedings of the First Conference of the Association of Southeast Asian Archaeologists in Western Europe, Institute of Archaeology, University College London, 8–10th September, 1986*, Eds Ian. Glover and Emily Glover. Oxford, BAR, 275–86.

Tan, Terence 2015. *Ancient Jewellery of Myanmar*, Shwe Htee Printing Press Yangoon, Myanmar.

Treloar, F.E., 1977. The Composition of Gold Artefacts from Santubong and Gedong, Sarawak. In *Sarawak Museum Journal* 25, no. 46:9–18.

Tucci, Antonino., Thongsa Sayavongkhamdy, Nigel Chang and Viengkeo Souksavatdy 2014. Ancient Copper Mining in Laos: Heterarchies, Incipient States or Post-State Anarchists? In: *Journal of Anthropology and Archaeology* December 2(2): 1–15.

Vallard, Annabel, Berenice Bellina-Pryce and Olivier Evrard, 2015. Cristalliser l'histoire: la seconde vie des perles préhistoriques en Thaïlande péninsulaire. *Artefact*: 189–203.

van Cutsem, Anne 2001. *A world of Earrings – Africa, Asia, America.* Skira editore, Milano.

Vo Si Khai 2003. The Kingdom of Fu Nan and the Culture of Oc Eo In *Art and Archaeology of Fu Nan: pre-Khmer Kingdom of the lower Mekong Valley*, Ed. J. C. M. Khoo. Bangkok, Orchid Press: 35 –86.

Wang, Gungwu 1958. The Nanhai Trade: A Study of the Early History of Chinese Trade in the South China Sea. In: *Journal of the Malayan Branch of the Royal Asiatic Society*, 31, 2: 1–135 (reprinted 1998 Singapore Times Academic Press).

Watson, William and Helmut Loofs 1967. The Thai-British Archaeological Expedition a preliminary report on the first season Journal of the Siam Society 55 (2): 237–62.

Wicks, Robert 1992. *Money, Markets, and Trade in Early Southeast Asia: The Development of Indigenous Monetary Systems to AD 1400.* Studies on Southeast Asia. Ithaca, NY: Southeast Asia Program, Cornell University.

White, Joyce and Vince Pigott 1996. From Community Craft to Regional Specialization: Intensification of Copper Production in Pre-State Thailand, in *Craft Specialization and Social Evolution: In memory of V. Gordon Childe*. Ed. B. Wailes. University Museum; Monograph 93. Philadelphia, PA: University Museum Publications: 151–175.